Twelve Jewish Steps To Recovery

A Personal Guide To Turning From Alcoholism And Other Addictions—Drugs, Food, Gambling, Sex...

Rabbi Kerry M. Olitzky

Stuart A. Copans, MD

Preface by Abraham J. Twerski, MD

Introduction by Rabbi Sheldon Zimmerman

Afterword by JACS

Illustrations by Maty Grünberg

16

EasyRead Large

RHYW

Copyright Page from the Original Book

Twelve Jewish Steps to Recovery, 2nd Edition:
A Personal Guide to Turning from Alcoholism and Other Addictions—Drugs, Food, Gambling, Sex ...

2009 Second Edition, Quality Paperback, First Printing
© 2009 by Kerry M. Olitzky and Stuart A. Copans

For information regarding permission to reprint material from this book, please mail or fax your request in writing to Jewish Lights Publishing, Permissions Department, at the address / fax number listed below, or e-mail your request to permissions@jewishlights.com.

The Library of Congress has cataloged the first edition as follows:
Olitzky, Kerry M.
Copans, Stuart A.
Twelve Jewish steps to recovery : a personal guide to turning from alcoholism and other addictions / Kerry M. Olitzky, Stuart A. Copans
      p.   cm.
ISBN-13: 978-1-879045-09-5 (quality pbk.)
ISBN-10: 1-879045-09-5 (quality pbk.)
1. Alcoholism—Religious aspects—Judaism. 2. Jews—Alcohol use. 3. Alcoholics—Rehabilitation. 4. Twelve-step programs—Religious aspects—Judaism. I. Copans, Stuart. II. Title.
HV5185.O45   1992
362.29'286'089924—dc20   91–25346

Second edition:
ISBN-13: 978-1-58023-409-2 (quality pbk.)
ISBN-10: 1-58023-409-7 (quality pbk.)

10 9 8 7 6 5 4 3 2 1

Manufactured in the United States of America

Cover design: Levavi & Levavi, modified by Melanie Robinson

Published by Jewish Lights Publishing
A Division of LongHill Partners, Inc.
Sunset Farm Offices, Route 4, P.O. Box 237
Woodstock, VT 05091
Tel: (802) 457-4000   Fax: (802) 457-4004
www.jewishlights.com

TABLE OF CONTENTS

Praise for Twelve Jewish Steps to Recovery, 2nd Edition i
Who Should Read This Book iv
The Jewish Lights Twelve Steps Series ix
Acknowledgments to the Second Edition xi
Acknowledgments to the First Edition xiii
Preface to the Second Edition xv
Preface to the First Edition xix
Introduction xxiii
How to Use This Book xxviii
The Twelve Steps of Alcoholics Anonymous xxix
The Hebrew Serenity Prayer xxxi

STEP ONE: HONESTY 1

STEP TWO: HOPE 11

STEP THREE: FAITH 20

STEP FOUR: COURAGE 31

STEP FIVE: INTEGRITY 41

STEP SIX: WILLINGNESS 55

STEP SEVEN: HUMILITY 65

STEP EIGHT: LOVE 76

STEP NINE: DISCIPLINE 85

STEP TEN: PERSEVERANCE 93

STEP ELEVEN: ILLUMINATION 101

STEP TWELVE: SERVICE 110

Moving from Here to Recovering: An Afterword 121

A Final Prayer 127

For Further Help 128

Notes 135

Glossary of Important Words and Concepts 138

Selected Readings 140

About the Illustrations 147

BACK COVER MATERIAL 167

Praise for Twelve Jewish Steps to Recovery, 2nd Edition

"An extremely valuable and helpful recovery tool. We are delighted to see it become available in a new edition, with added material from contemporary Jewish spiritual leaders! This is a much loved and highly useful book."

—*Jonathan Katz, LCSW*
JACS (Jewish Alcoholics, Chemically Dependent Persons and Significant Others), a program of the Jewish Board of Family and Children's Services

"A must-read for every Jew desiring a road map to living a life of decency, wholeness and Truth. Brings together the path to wholeness through Judaic spiritual principles and the Twelve Steps of Alcoholics Anonymous better than any other book I have read."

—*Rabbi Mark Borovitz*
coauthor, *The Holy Thief: A Con Man's Journey from Darkness to Light*

"Essential to many individuals in their initial and ongoing work of recovery as well as to the professionals in the Jewish community who partner with them to change our attitudes and our institutions. The expanded second edition adds meaningful words and updated resources to enhance the spiritual journey of all those who want to transform their lives."

—*Rabbi Stephanie Dickstein, LMSW*
spiritual care coordinator, Shira Ruskay Center, The Jewish Board of Family and Children's Services

"User-friendly.... [A] step-by-step formula that enables and empowers the reader to deal with and overcome formidable and often overwhelming demons that might otherwise be ignored or denied."

—*Stephen S. Pearce,*
PhD senior rabbi, Congregation Emanu-El of San Francisco

"Addictions in the Jewish community have remained hidden for far too long.... This book is the first aimed directly at helping the addicted person and family. Everyone affected or interested should read it."

—*Sheila B. Blume, MD, CAC*

medical director, Alcoholism, Chemical Dependency and Compulsive Gambling Programs, South Oaks Hospital

"If I were to recommend one book on the experience of addictive behavior, it would be this one ... because it is universally authentic, compassionate, and life-enhancing."
—Rabbi Earl A. Grollman, DD
author, *Living When a Loved One Has Died* and *In Sickness and in Health*

"I read *Twelve Jewish Steps* with the eyes of a Christian and came away renewed in my heart. I felt like I had visited my Jewish roots. These authors have deep knowledge of recovery as viewed by Alcoholics Anonymous."
—Rock J. Stack, MA, LLD
manager, Clinical–Pastoral Education, Hazelden Foundation

"Recommended reading for people of all denominations."
—Abraham J. Twerski, MD
medical director emeritus and founder, Gateway Treatment Center

Who Should Read This Book

This book is not just for Jewish people. It is for all people who would gain strength to heal and insight from Jewish tradition.

✓ Anyone who is seeking an understanding of the Twelve Steps from a Jewish perspective—regardless of religious background or affiliation

✓ Alcoholics and addicts in recovery and all people who are in trouble with alcohol and drugs and other addictions—food, gambling, and sex

• Affiliated Jews: Reform, Conservative, Reconstructionist, Orthodox

• All other Jews who seek guidance from a shared and sacred tradition

• People of all faiths who seek both guidance and renewal through recovery

✓ Codependents

• Anyone who is in an addictive relationship

• Anyone who was raised in a dysfunctional family

• Adult children of alcoholics

✓ Specialists in Recovery

• Friends who care

• Rabbis, priests and ministers, spiritual counselors of all kinds

- Alcohol and chemical dependency counselors
- Psychiatrists, psychologists, therapists

The first step says it all; it establishes a foundation for everything else. Alcohol (or drugs, eating, sex, or gambling) is making a mess of your life because you are addicted or care deeply about someone who is. Even if you are not addicted or do not know someone who is, this book will offer you the inspiration to face the challenges of life and daily living. In one broad admission, the first step epitomizes the entire Twelve Step program. This process of recovery has proven itself effective for thousands of people—providing they worked the program. Each step is worked through over and over again, moving us forward in recovery every time we move through the steps, whether simultaneously or one at a time.

As Jews we are taught that God spoke at Mount Sinai in 600,000 voices—one for each Israelite who had fled Egyptian slavery, surrounding Sinai, waiting for God's revelation. Six hundred thousand voices, so that each individual could understand in his or her own way.

Such is the case with this guide. Many Jewish voices are heard in each step. Religious voices, humanist voices, and just plain people's voices. Search out your own. You will find it in these pages. It will speak to you throughout all of Jewish tradition. Listen for it. It will ring loud and clear during the entire recovery process and help you on your way to recovery.

It is hard to give up addictions. Words do not adequately express the difficulty. There is a certain comfort in addiction and in the denial of our dependence. Usually only some severe trauma, some near-catastrophic event, makes us realize how low and desperate we have become. Listen to the words of one who wants to share:

Even as a child I remember having problems with alcohol. For Kiddush (blessing over wine) my wine glass always had to be overflowing. One did not hold back from making a blessing, even if the overflow was drunk from the saucer. If a blessing over wine was good, a blessing over whiskey was beneficial as well. Drinking was for the sake of fulfilling another *mitzvah* (divine commandment), and another, and yet another. *Yiddishkeit* (ethnic Jewish identity) included *Bronfe, Mehd* and Schnapps along with wine. And what was Passover without *Shlivovitz?* We Jews have a rich variety of alcohol in our culture. I never thought I was an alcoholic. As a child I would pass out at a Passover Seder. But this was cute, because I was a "happy little drunk." This happened also at a Sukkot celebration or Simchat Torah or Purim. I remember as a child going around drinking the cups left by adults at a *simcha* (happy occasion) in *shul* (synagogue). Didn't everyone do that? I had one great-uncle who ruined a career as a talented violinist because he began to show up at concerts too drunk to perform. We all thought it was hilarious when we had to fish Uncle Zalman out of the bathtub after he drank too much at my brother's Bar Mitzvah. But *shikker* was always a *goy....*

Jews are addicted in our community. Face it. We have. This book is here to help. We are here to help. Come journey to recovery with us. Together, we will try to save your life, nothing less.

The Holy Blessed One built a Jerusalem above in the likeness of the one below but has made an oath not to enter heavenly Jerusalem until first entering earthly Jerusalem.

(Zohar 1:80b, 3:15b)

The Jewish Lights Twelve Steps Series

100 Blessings Every Day
Daily Twelve Step Recovery Affirmations, Exercises for Personal Growth & Renewal Reflecting Seasons of the Jewish Year
By Rabbi Kerry M. Olitzky

Recovery from Codependence
A Jewish Twelve Steps Guide to Healing Your Soul
By Rabbi Kerry M. Olitzky

Renewed Each Day
Daily Twelve Step Recovery Meditations Based on the Bible (Volume I—Genesis & Exodus; Volume 2—Leviticus, Numbers & Deuteronomy)
By Rabbi Kerry M. Olitzky and Aaron Z.

Twelve Jewish Steps to Recovery, 2nd Edition
A Personal Guide to Turning from Alcoholism & Other Addictions—Drugs, Food, Gambling, Sex...

By Rabbi Kerry M. Olitzky and Stuart A Copans, MD

ALSO AVAILABLE

Recovery—The Sacred Art
The Twelve Steps as Spiritual Practice
By Rami Shapiro
(A book from SkyLight Paths, Jewish Lights' sister imprint)

Acknowledgments to the Second Edition

There have been many people who have contributed to this new edition, whether or not their names or words are specifically included. It is because of them that there is a demand for a new edition of this book, and I thank all of them.

I also want to thank once again Stuart and Antoinette Matlins, whose vision for Jewish Lights Publishing extends far beyond our reach and thereby pushes us all to greater heights and depths. There is no better publishing staff with which to work, as well. So I thank all of my friends and colleagues at Jewish Lights Publishing, particularly Emily Wichland, Elizabeth Martin, Lauren Hill, and Kate Treworgy, who, each in their own individual way, helped to make sure that my words say what I want them to say, and that they reach those who need to hear them to be uplifted and inspired and to find support in their individual recovery.

I also want to thank my colleagues at the Jewish Outreach Institute, where I am privileged to do the work I am called to do each day.

I have included new, contemporary voices for recovery in this volume. So I thank the following people for allowing me to share their insights and wisdom in these pages so that others may benefit: Rabbi Norman J. Cohen, Merle Feld, Rabbi Daniel Gordis, Rabbi Karyn D. Kedar, Rabbi Harold Kushner, Rabbi Lawrence Kushner, Rabbi Shoni Labowitz, Rabbi Jonathan Magonet, Carol Ochs, Rabbi Harold M. Schulweis, Rabbi Rami Shapiro, Rabbi Ira F. Stone, and Rabbi David Wolpe.

I am blessed to be supported by a wonderful family: my wife and best friend Sheryl, my sons Avi and Jesse, and their life partners and soul-mates, Sarah and Andrea, who have entered our lives and our family since the first edition of this volume. As folk wisdom has it, love knows no bounds. It continues to grow as our family expands.

Rabbi Kerry M. Olitzky

Acknowledgments to the First Edition

Behind each word in this book are heard many voices. Some of these voices choose to remain anonymous. Others we wish to recognize and thank. While there are far too many people to mention by name, we do want to express abiding appreciation to our colleagues and friends at JACS (Jewish Alcoholics, Chemically Dependent Persons, and Significant Others), a program of the Jewish Board of Family and Children's Services (formerly the JACS Foundation) in New York City, who have opened up their lives to us and taken us along with them on their journeys in recovery. In particular, we thank Jeff Neipris and David Buchholz.

Those at Hebrew Union College–Jewish Institute of Religion in New York, at the Fabrangen Community in Washington, DC, and at the Brattleboro Retreat in Brattleboro, Vermont, who labor with us in our own spiritual and clinical quests deserve special recognition. In particular, we thank Norman Cohen and Linda Jaffe; we also thank David Shneyer, Nick Belsky, Jill Gentilin, Elizabeth Reasoner, and Barbara Uhrie.

Our editor, David Szonyi, turned thoughts into words. We owe him our gratitude. We also express our gratitude for the creative insights of our colleague Lawrence Hoffman, who brought this idea to Jewish Lights. And our publishers, Stuart and Antoinette Matlins and Jevin Eagle, have helped make this labor of love soar heavenward. This volume would not be possible without them. Our words are their words.

Finally, we feel richly blessed by spouses and children who nurture our deeds and thoughts everyday that we live: Sheryl, Avi, and Jesse Olitzky and Mary, Laurie, Roy, Jon, and Ben Copans. It is because of them that our words and lives find profound meaning in this world and beyond.

Rabbi Kerry M. Olitzky
Stuart A. Copans, MD

Preface to the Second Edition

The relationship between the organized Jewish community and Jews in recovery has changed dramatically since we conceived and wrote this book almost twenty years ago. There are a variety of factors that contributed to these changes. Among them was that, about the same time as this book was published, I helped to organize the first formal training program in North America for rabbis and cantors in the area of substance abuse and recovery. It was a joint project between various liberal rabbinical seminaries (Hebrew Union College–Jewish Institute of Religion, Jewish Theological Seminary, and the Reconstructionist Rabbinical College) and the JACS Foundation, Inc., which is now known as JACS (Jewish Alcoholics, Chemically Dependent Persons, and Significant Others), a program of the Jewish Board of Family and Children's Services in New York City. Since that time, participants in the program—rabbis and cantors, as well as student rabbis and cantors, many of them just starting out in the field—took what they learned and quickly implemented it at the institutions and organizations they led. Moreover, they influenced attitudes about those in recovery and shattered many myths, particularly among other Jewish communal professionals and volunteer leaders.

And they helped literally to open doors that were previously closed to those in recovery, especially to Twelve Step groups desirous of meeting at synagogues and Jewish Community Centers and other Jewish communal institutions. And the JACS Foundation extended its influence with satellite and derivative programs throughout the United States and in Israel, often in communities where these rabbis and cantors live and work.

This book also led to the development of the entire Twelve Step Recovery Series published by Jewish Lights Publishing and the expansion of an entire genre of spiritual recovery literature in the Jewish community. It was an attempt to build a bridge from the vast treasure house of Jewish sacred sources and those who sought spiritual insight and direction for their recovery from it, often without the tools to access these sources on their own. But the revision of this book specifically emerged out of the articulated request of numerous people, including some of those from the original JACS group in New York who introduced me to the world of their recovery, to update the material included in it. They simply wanted more and felt that this was the best way to get it. But when I asked people about such changes and improvements for the revised edition, particularly those who work the steps daily and who use this book regularly to assist them in their recovery, or with the recovery of others, they asked me not to change anything in the book. They didn't want to alter something that they felt was indispensable to their recovery and personal growth. So we reached a compromise. While this book contains the same material as the original edition—even as it evolved through eight subsequent printings—it has been updated and expanded to include additional readings, resources, and pages to record your own personal reflections at the end of each chapter. It also includes new references for a variety of Jewish residential treatment centers that were not in operation when the first edition was published.

Much learning has taken place since the time of the original introduction of this book. Many of the principles that I learned in putting these ideas on paper contributed to the growing literature of contemporary Jewish spirituality and synagogue reform. As I have frequently said, if all members of the Jewish community practiced the implicit behaviors in many of the steps, our synagogues would be full and we would indeed be closer to *mashiach-zeit* (the time of the Messiah).

So the sum of these pages is more than just a book, more than even the all-important collection of life-saving strategies for recovery. This book reflects an entire movement that forced a paradigm shift in the way the Jewish community responds to those in recovery from alcoholism and other addictions, as well as compulsive behaviors. As a result, this book holds its rightful place along the path to paving a way to a better world.

Rabbi Kerry M. Olitzky

Preface to the First Edition

The most serious public health problem of this generation—substance abuse, which includes alcoholism and both licit and illicit drug addiction with their many and varied sequelae—is indeed a problem that poses a challenge to the Jewish community. The only reason for making this observation is the intense denial within the Jewish community, as expressed in the Yiddish aphorism *"shikker* is a *goy"* (A drunk, a Gentile is), a statement that has now been amply disproven. Drug addiction, whether to prescribed or "street" drugs, never did qualify for the assumed immunity, yet here too denial prevails within the Jewish community.

A further difficulty is that even when denial is finally overcome, there is much resistance to the most effective treatment modality for these conditions: the Twelve Step programs of Alcoholics Anonymous (AA), Narcotics Anonymous (NA), and their respective family groups. Reasons for resisting participation in AA and NA are legion,[1] and Jews have added a potent resistance to the list: "AA and NA are Christian programs, and Jews are not permitted to participate in them."

It is true that AA had its origin in the Oxford Group, who were Christian fundamentalists. However, the principles of AA and NA as presented in Twelve Steps are not in any way non-Jewish. To the contrary, all of the Twelve Steps can be found in the Talmud and traditional Torah works.

Olitzky and Copans have made a major contribution in this delightful book, wherein they demonstrate conclusively that the Twelve Steps are very, very Jewish. The material is presented succinctly and with great lucidity, and no one can claim that it is too esoteric for the layperson. After reading this book, no one can legitimately argue that the Twelve Step programs are alien to Judaism.

There will undoubtedly be those who will say, "Yes, but..." and will point to the majority of AA/NA meetings being held in church basements and the traditional recitation of the Lord's Prayer as evidence of the Christian character of these programs. It should be evident that the reason meetings are generally held in churches rather than in synagogues is precisely because the Jewish community never considered addiction to be its problem. Insofar as the Lord's Prayer is concerned, it is not an integral part of the Twelve Step program, and everyone is free to chose his/her own prayer. Some of the prayers cited by the authors in this book are particularly appropriate for people in recovery.

If there is any lingering doubt as to the universal application of the Twelve Steps, let me point out a simple fact. Under what circumstances would you ever find an *Orthodox, Hasidic* rabbi recommending without reservation a treatise on spirituality written by a *Reform* rabbi and another psychiatrist? It should be clear that if rabbis representing denominations that have major differences in their respective positions are unanimous in the espousal of the Twelve Steps, there is no conceivable reason to object to them on religious grounds.

Addictive behavior of any type, whether to alcohol, drugs, foods, sex, or gambling, is often a manifestation of maladjustment to life situations. Needless to say, there are many other types of maladjustment that are not of an addictive character. The same Twelve Steps that have proven so effective in recovery from addictions can also be helpful in avoiding or correcting other maladjustments, and Olitzky and Copan's presentation of the Twelve Steps should therefore be of value to persons who have problems that do not involve any specific addiction.

In addition to demonstrating the compatibility and indeed the Jewish character of the Twelve Steps, the authors have also elucidated them in a manner that make this book recommended reading for people of all denominations.

Abraham J. Twerski, MD
Founder and Medical Director Emeritus
Gateway Rehabilitation Center

Aliquippa, Pennsylvania

Introduction

My first serious encounter as a rabbi with the problem of Jewish alcoholism and Jewish alcoholics took place during my first year in the rabbinate. A member of Central Synagogue, my former congregation in New York, called on the telephone saying that she had to see me as soon as possible. We met that very day. She indicated to me that her husband was an alcoholic and that whenever she had told me and her friends that her husband was on a business trip he had actually been drying out in a rehab center. I was startled and confused. I told her that I had never seen him drink. In all the times we had been together socially or in the congregation, I had never seen him with a drink in his hand. Naively, I had asserted that he couldn't be an alcoholic. She smiled and explained that he never drank socially or at home. He only drank at work.

This brave and heroic woman was taking a risk. She had received her husband's permission to tell me the truth. She instinctively felt that I would not turn her away and that I would be responsive to a simple request she would make. She told me that there were many Jewish alcoholics and that she and her husband hoped that I would join them on a six-month voyage of discovery. They would take me to AA meetings, Al-Anon meetings, and Alateen meetings throughout Manhattan. They would introduce me to their acquaintances and friends in AA. If I would be willing, Jewish members of AA would come to speak with me. For six months they took me by the hand, and I received my primary lessons about alcoholism and about the extraordinary number of Jews who are alcoholics.

The rest is history. Central Synagogue was the first synagogue to host an AA group. The Federation of Jewish Philanthropies of New York established the first task force on Jewish alcoholism. Out of that task force came the retreats that led to the founding of JACS. The programs have been numerous, the impact national and international. What extraordinary years these have been.

I was privileged and blessed to be one of the first rabbis to work with, counsel, and be taught by Jewish alcoholics. In those first five years alone, I counseled and met with hundreds of Jewish alcoholics. From them I learned so much about life, about faith, and about the presence of the living God as an essential part of life. Through them, the words of prayer took on more profound significance. In their agony and in their healing, faith became a primary category.

The alcoholics I worked with came from a variety of Jewish backgrounds, some very traditional, some secular, but most from

Conservative and Reform backgrounds. Most were unobservant at the time that I met with them. Interestingly, a few were Hasidic as well. Those from more liberal backgrounds talked about how unprepared they were as Jews for the faith demands and process of the Twelve Steps. They knew a lot about Jewish history and holidays, but very little about God. The synagogues and temples they attended were active places, but lacked spiritual depth and meaning in their eyes. They felt that the services left them untouched and that the rabbis preached about everything but God. I never argued with them about their perceptions. After all, their perceptions were real for them, and they were desperate for spiritual contact.

As a liberal rabbi and a liberal Jew, I find that the encounter with Jewish alcoholics and alcoholism and the Twelve Step program of AA has proven essential to my growth and becoming. Liberal Judaism as practiced in this country has often centered around ethnicity, folk traditions, social and political activism, social justice, and community philanthropy. Much of our Jewish energy has been spent in these areas. For many of us the burning fire of faith, although desired, was an unknown. We found ourselves removed from the flame of the burning bush that Moses encountered. We envied the spiritual vibrancy and passion of other movements in Judaism. For whatever reason, spirituality was not a part of our daily or weekly Jewish existence.

The beauty and significance of the Twelve Step program is that it enables us and those with whom we work to find a Jewish center of spirit and faith in our lives. Integrating the Twelve Steps with the profound teachings of Jewish tradition and faith and with the traditional process of *teshuvah* (repentance and return) enables liberal Jews to find a program that puts into an understandable and doable process the search for the world of the spirit and a personal relationship with God.

I never left a counseling session untouched by God's presence. I have stood before the Holy Ark many times as Jewish alcoholics have prayed or confessed or let go. I have wept with them, I have been angry with them, I have been enriched spiritually to the very depth of my being. I know that this has been the case with other liberal rabbis and Jews as well. We have grown far away from some of the sources of our faith. We, too, need a way back and in. That unique combination of Judaism and the Twelve Steps takes us by the hand and guides us to possibilities and affirmations of belief that few of us thought possible. We transcend all the barriers and stand at the burning bush and at Sinai once again.

Rabbi Sheldon Zimmerman
Founder of the Task Force

*on Alcoholism of the UJA-
Federation of New York*

How to Use This Book

This book requires a special kind of reading. You don't have to sit and read it cover to cover, or even start at the beginning. Flip through the pages. Read a little at a time, over and over, if you like. Read a step a day, or a step a week, or a step a month—whatever works for you. Just read it. And get others to read it also. Together we can all find strength from the Twelve Steps and our Jewish tradition.

Surely this instruction which I enter into covenant with you today is not too much to comprehend, nor is it beyond your grasp. It is not in heaven, to prevent you from saying, "Who from among us can go to heaven and get it for us and teach it to us so that we may comply with it?"

Neither is it across the seas to prevent you from saying, "Who from among us can get to the other side of the sea and get it for us and teach it to us so that we may behave in accordance with it?"

No. This teaching is very close to your mouth, in your heart, so that you may observe it.

Deuteronomy 30:11–14

The Twelve Steps of Alcoholics Anonymous

The twelve steps are reprinted and adapted with permission of Alcoholics Anonymous World Services, Inc. Permission to reprint and adapt the Twelve Steps does not mean that AA is affiliated with this program. AA is a program of recovery from alcoholism—use of the Twelve Steps in connection with programs and activities that are patterned after AA but that address other problems does not imply otherwise.[2]

1. We admitted we were powerless over alcohol—that our lives had become unmanageable.
2. Came to believe that a Power greater than ourselves could restore us to sanity.
3. Made a decision to turn our will and our lives over to the care of God as we understood Him.
4. Made a searching and fearless moral inventory of ourselves.
5. Admitted to God, to ourselves, and to another human being the exact nature of our wrongs.
6. Were entirely ready to have God remove all these defects of character.
7. Humbly asked Him to remove our shortcomings.

8. Made a list of all persons we had harmed, and became willing to make amends to them all.

9. Made direct amends to such people wherever possible, except when to do so would injure them or others.

10 Continued to take personal inventory and when we were wrong promptly admitted it.

11. Sought through prayer and meditation to improve our conscious contact with God as we understood Him, praying only for knowledge of His will for us and the power to carry that out.

12. Having had a spiritual awakening as a result of these Steps, we tried to carry this message to alcoholics, and to practice these principles in all our affairs.

The Hebrew Serenity Prayer

Ey-li teyn li et hashalvah
L'kabeyl et had'varim sheh'eyn b'yacholti
l'shanotam
Ohmetz l'shanot et had'varim asher
b'yacholti
Ut'vunah l'havcheen baynayhem

God, grant me the serenity
to accept the things I cannot change
courage to change the things I can
and wisdom to know the difference

STEPPED AND ARCHED IN THE HILLY OLD CITY OF JERUSALEM

STEP ONE

HONESTY

We admitted we were powerless over alcohol—that our lives had become unmanageable.

- We. Not them. Us. That means we are in this together.
- No more denial, blaming others, pretending.
- Your dependency is controlling your life. It is wreaking havoc everywhere. Admit it.
- Dependency is a problem. Face the facts. It is messing up your life, hurting you and those who love you.
- This simple admission gives us the power to get on the road to recovery.

By reading these lines, you have already taken the first and most important step in recovery. All first steps are difficult. We understand that. Everyone understands that. That is why we and many people in your life are here to help.

You are following in the footsteps of our ancestors in this brave beginning. When our people were poised at the Red Sea, the

Egyptian armies in hot pursuit, they panicked. The Israelites were afraid to cross. Moses cajoled them, but to no avail. Fearful that they had come so far only to perish in the waters, our ancestors were ready to return to Egypt and again become enslaved. This may also be our fear. We stand at the threshold of the Red Sea every day struggling, fighting the urge to return to the slavery of our dependency.

One man arose, Nachshon ben Aminadav, a simple man, neither hero nor leader, and stepped into the raging waters. Then a miracle occurred. The waters parted, and these former slaves walked on dry land toward freedom.

You too must be willing to take the first step. Others will persuade you, even try to help you. But the miracle of recovery is not possible until you can take the first step yourself. Then the miracle of recovery will begin for you.

Our sages teach that the process of repentance, of turning and reawakening, begins with the act of seeing ourselves clearly, with all our imperfections. Our recovery begins when we give up on denial, when we admit to our powerlessness over addictions, when we see how utterly unmanageable our lives have become.

The "we" is important. Both Judaism and AA emphasize community and the support it offers each member. As Jews, we move through history as a community, in prayer, celebration, even sorrow. Remember the "bad" child of the four in the Passover Haggadah, the liturgical book used during the Passover ritual meal? That child was considered "bad," some even called him "evil" or "wicked," because he said, "God did not do anything for *me. I was not there."* But it was *we* as an entire people who went through slavery and were liberated; *we* who must remember.

Listen to the words of someone who does remember: "I'll never forget the last seder before I got help. *Zeyde* (grandfather) was leading us in listing aloud the Ten Plagues, and suddenly I began to see my own: alcohol, cocaine, dishonesty, neglect."

This admission is like the confessional prayers of the High Holidays. *We* ask for forgiveness for all we have done or said to profane our lives. This use of "we" binds us as a group. *We* all sinned. *We* are in this together.

Feeling part of a small group—a *minyan* (prayer quorum) or a *chavura* (extended family-like social group) in community life—is a basic human need. Perhaps you used alcohol or drugs to become part of a group. That's the past. Now you might rejoin the Jewish group. You will gain strength from it. Attend worship services regularly. Volunteer to help or serve on a committee. Whatever you do, go to a local synagogue and join in. Go to AA meetings too. Get there early. Make coffee. Set up chairs. Stay late.

Choose a sponsor and a teacher. If you really look, you'll find both. There's no real mystery to it. It may feel like a conscious choice or an inspiration. Our tradition says that "when a student is ready, a teacher will appear."

But don't just wait for it to happen. Take an active role in choosing an AA meeting, in selecting a rabbi to be your spiritual counselor, to guide you and help you find your place in the Jewish community.

We don't want to kid you. Recovery will be a difficult journey, filled with success, failure—and disappointment. Remember, it took our people forty years, an entire generation, of wandering in the desert before we were able to reach the promised land. We had to rid ourselves of the slave mentality.

With each leg of the journey there arose obstacles to be endured and overcome. You have to do the same thing. First, you shake the addiction, then the self-perception of an addict.

Since we delude ourselves into believing that we control so much in our lives and in the world, we are terrified at the prospect of not being in control. As a people, we know what it is like to feel powerless. How often have we been forced to move throughout our history, often feeling helpless to shape our own destiny?

Our grandparents! In the darkness of night, they packed their bags and fled in fear for their lives and those of their families. Yet, somehow our people always have known that they had to take the first step if they were to improve their lot. Powerlessness does not have to be passivity.

As Jews, we do not believe in chaos. Rather, order is what anchors us in this world. For countless generations, Jewish teachers have argued that the world was created according to an orderly plan.

Look out your window. The sun will rise and set each day. One season will evolve into another. Count on it. Likewise, our tradition teaches us that we are created anew each day, as is the world, giving both the opportunity to start afresh.

When the world we have built and the family we have nurtured are threatened because of our dependence, we should act. Do we have to wait until they are destroyed as a result of our addiction before we are ready to give up that to which we're addicted? No. Don't wait. Do it now. When we admit that we are powerless, that order may be restored in our lives—as part of the way the world works, and we can count on it—we begin to live again, experiencing rebirth and renewal.

As we will see in Step Two, when we are ready to trust the orderliness of the world once again, things will happen to affirm that trust.

HELP FROM OUR TRADITION

Nothing remains the same; everything blossoms, everything ascends, everything steadily increases in light and truth. The enlightened spirit does not become discouraged even when it discerns that the path of ascendance is circuitous, including both advance and decline, a forward movement but also fierce retreats, for even our retreats abound in the potential of future progress.

Rabbi Abraham Isaac Kook

SOMETHING TO THINK ABOUT

Find yourself a teacher and acquire for yourself a colleague and friend.

Pirke Avot 1:6

TOWARD SOBRIETY, A PSALM

Your anger may last only for a moment
Your favor a lifetime
Tears may linger at evening
but in the morning comes joy.

Psalm 30:6

TEFILLAT HA-DERECH (PRAYER SAID UPON EMBARKING ON A JOURNEY)

May it be Your will, Adonai,[3] my God and God of my ancestors, to lead me, to direct my steps, and to support me in peace. Lead me in life, tranquil and serene, until I arrive at where I am going. Deliver me from every enemy, ambush and hurt that I might encounter on the way, and from all afflictions that visit and trouble the world.

Bless the work of my hands. Let me receive divine grace and those loving acts of kindness and mercy in Your eyes and in the eyes of all those I encounter. Listen to the voice of my appeal, for You are a God who responds to prayerful supplication. Praised are You, Adonai, who responds to prayer. Amen.

CONTEMPORARY VOICES FOR RECOVERY

In some ways, life is all about coping with loss—from the first time the breast is withdrawn from our hungry mouths to our last farewells. The rabbis suggested that when we are born our hands are clenched as if we wish to grasp the entire world, and when we die they are open, as we give everything up. That life is a constant giving up is so obvious that we know it in different ways at all times—but it is so unacceptable in the rush and energy of life that it catches us unawares every time.

Rabbi Jonathan Magonet[4]

REFLECTIONS

_____

_____

_____

M. GRÜNBERG / ZION GATE / JERUSALEM
OPPOSITE MOUNT ZION

STEP TWO

HOPE

Came to believe that a power greater than ourselves could restore us to sanity.

> • Believing in a Power greater than ourselves is a choice we make.
> • Making this choice begins the process of recovery.
> • At this stage it may be simple, concrete things or people that help us take this step.

As Jews we may be uncomfortable when we first consider Step Two. We may hear it as claiming that we are not responsible for what happens to us, that we will be helped or saved by something or someone outside of ourselves who does it for us. Some of us even hear it as "salvation" in a Christian sense, with someone redeeming us. It can be very uncomfortable. We turn off, shut down, feel threatened.

But first, we have to see that the step says "could restore us to sanity," not will. The movement from "could" to "will," from potential to actual, depends on us.

Whether or not you decide to believe in a Power that is greater than yourself is a choice that you make. You decide. We decided. And, you even get to decide—or maybe it would be better to say *have* to decide—just what that Power is.

For our part, we know that God exists. For you, that Power may be less defined, less specific, less real. But to move ahead to sanity, you simply have to take that one step that moves you outside the trap of yourself, of total self-involvement. One addict in recovery explained, "I never thought of myself as a religious person. It was because the dope was clogging my mind and my spirit." It doesn't matter whether it is God with a long white beard, or with a woman's form, a vague cloud, or anything else you can imagine. It only matters that there is something or someone there beyond and beside you. You just have to decide you want to connect with it.

When you make that decision, you have taken a step that leads you not only to God, but also to the other important people in your life—family, friends, an AA sponsor—who will also help you to restore your sanity.

When our biblical ancestor Joseph was looking for his brothers in Dothan, he wandered, lost, until he chanced upon an unnamed person who helped him find his way. Joseph could not find it on his own. Rabbi Menachem Mendl, a great nineteenth-century Hasidic rebbe, teaches that when Joseph's soul cried out from the depths of despair inside him, he was struggling to know what he really wanted and yearned for. Only by knowing this would he be able to return to his path in life. Only then would his vision actually become his path.

Like Joseph, we find ourselves confused about our life's path and so turn to alcohol, drugs, food, sex, and gambling. But even Joseph did not realize until much later in his life, after he became Pharaoh's viceroy, that neither he nor the brothers who had sold him into slavery really were in control. God had a plan for Joseph's life; he merely had to find it.

We Jews always have known that belief is essential—but that doesn't mean it is easy. If you are struggling with belief, you have lots of company now and throughout our long history. In fact, our tradition tells us, the one power God withholds even from Godself is the power to make us believe. But hard doesn't mean impossible. "Not yet" isn't never, and difficulty in faith isn't failure.

Look at the golden calf incident, where we turned our backs on God after all God did for us in bringing us out of Egypt. But God hadn't done anything for us lately. How far is it from the golden calf to the heroin addict's golden arm[5] or the compulsive gambler's lost money? Our sages knew that the distance was very short. In fact, perhaps there is no difference between the golden calf and the golden arm.

The sages pointed out that there are many kinds and forms of golden calves in our lives.

HELP FROM OUR TRADITION

Abba Mieri taught in the name of the Baal Shem Tov, "For even the one who is occupied with the daily pursuits of business, when the time arrives for afternoon prayers, he hurries, sighing, praying with a broken heart. This sigh alone pierces the heavens."

SOMETHING TO THINK ABOUT

Rabbi Meir said: "Study with all your heart and with all of your soul to know God's ways and to watch at the doors of the Divine law. Keep God's law in your heart and let Divine reverence always be before your eyes. Keep your mouth from sin and purify and sanctify yourself from trespass and iniquity and God will be with you in every place."

Babylonian Talmud, Berachot 17a

A MEDITATION

Live by the commandments; do not die by them.

Babylonian Talmud, Sanhedrin 7a

TOWARD SOBRIETY, A PSALM

Fortunate is the person who has not followed
the plan of the wicked,
or participated with sinners.
or joined the company of scoffers.
Rather, his desire is the teaching of
Adonai,
and he meditates on that teaching
all the time.
He is like a tree firmly planted
beside abundant waters
that yields its fruit in season
whose foliage never withers
and whatever he does prospers.

Psalm 1:1-3

A PRAYER

In desperation, I call out to You for help and guidance through this trying, tumultuous, painful whirlwind of confusion. I find myself haunted with emotions that are unbearably ridden with guilt and endless introspective questioning of who I have become. My hungry soul is starving for the answers to satiate its craving for comfort and contentment.

The agony is no longer at a surface level but has embedded itself deep within the innermost layers of my being. The dagger of denial is piercing deeper and deeper through the confines of my essence, and the scars are becoming more difficult to conceal.

I pray for Your assistance in easing this excruciating torment that I have afflicted myself with. I must realize, though, that all I can expect from You is Your guidance. I, alone, must labor to create my transformation.

The courage to change is the most trying, difficult and challenging task that has ever been set before me. I now realize that, step by step, with Your infinite love, patience and wisdom, I can take hold of the serenity I so long to grasp. With belief and trust in You, my precious God, everything is within my reach. At times, however, I must lift up my arms and outstretch my hands just a little bit further.

Esther L.
Queens, NY

CONTEMPORARY VOICES FOR RECOVERY

Praise of God exalts the ideal for our own spiritual character. Praise of God serves as the benchmark against which we judge the conduct of our life, and, at times, even the ways of God. The ideal of the divine may give rise to a reproach of God.... Covenantal prayer is neither subservient nor imperious. It opens a two-way bridge on which I and Thou may meet.

Rabbi Harold M. Schulweis[6]

REFLECTIONS

M. GRÜNZWEIG / THE LION GATE

STEP THREE

FAITH

Made a decision to turn our will and our lives over to the care of God as we understand God.

- Decisions shape our lives and determine how we grow.
- The very act of deciding means that you begin to take back control of your life.
- When you change who you are, trying to become what you might be, you enter sacred time and sacred space. There, the old you slowly evolves into the new person you yearn to become.
- This decision may take the form of an enormous leap. Don't be afraid to make it. It's all part of getting sober and whole again.
- The way you live your life, and the decisions you make, reflect your understanding of and relationship with God.
- As much as we think that we can go it alone, especially after a little success on the road to recovery, we find that God is truly the source of our spiritual nourishment, inspiring us to move forward.

When alcohol or drugs cloud your mind and paralyze you, distorting your decision-making ability, you no longer are in control. Once you again begin making decisions, you may hesitate, feel uncertain, make mistakes. But once you get going, it will seem like the smoothest ride you've taken in a long time.

But that good feeling also is somewhat illusory. You'll still feel plenty of bumps. When you leave the person you know so well to become the person you really want to be, it's very scary. You may well want to turn back, to return to Egypt. Don't be afraid to be frightened—it's very much part of recovery.

Some people think that faith in God comes easily: You wake up one day and BAM! it hits you. No way. For Jews, belief in God is a struggle. We spend our lives trying to figure out the range and shape of that belief, what it means, how it compels us to act.

Just start by deciding that you will try to believe. You will have doubts; we all do. You will have days when you think that God is everywhere. You might spend days thinking that God is completely hidden from the world. When you see injustices, you may be angry and defiant. Somehow, keep struggling, keep working at it. Ultimately, your belief will breathe fresh life into your soul. This is the way one friend put it: "My soul was empty and I tried to fill it with food. It didn't work."

Throughout the Jewish calendar year, we are given opportunities to start again, to make *teshuvah,* a turning, to turn toward God and the path of routine life. Yes, *routine,* nothing special, a regular life.

For the entire month of Elul (around late August or September, depending on the year), before Rosh Hashanah (Jewish New Year) and Yom Kippur (Day of Atonement), the birthing of the world and the day of ultimate decision, we prepare ourselves. We get ready for the day that each year symbolizes, that moment when we shed our past and begin our journey toward personal repair. The very beginning of Scripture captures this time when fearfulness and bleakness can be transformed: "When God began to create ... the world was chaotic, without order. And so, God drew near to the chaos and brought light to the world in order to illumine the darkness" (Genesis 1:1–4).

Here, at this place, you take the third step of your journey. Just as the creation of life is a process of growth, so too is the process of recovery. With each moment of living sober, free from addiction, you grow stronger, both in purpose and in resolve.

Stepping back from the canvas of creation, God recognized that the finishing touches were missing. Instead of raising again the artist's brush, God paused and handed it to us, placing the final responsibility of ongoing creation in our hands. We have much work yet to do. We are not talking about large things like mountains and rivers. No—even greater things like you and your life and the love and respect of your family and friends and colleagues. God is not going to do all the work. You are God's partner.

Get to know God, before you are ready to turn anything over. Use prayer and meditation. Create in Shabbat, the Sabbath, a place of peace and refuge for yourself. Music and poetry can help too, especially *niggunim,* the wordless chants of the *Hasidim,* Orthodox Jews who passionately serve God, easily discernible by their long black coats and hanging side curls.

This adult child of alcoholics found God: "After a year and a half of therapy, I was strong enough to go to Israel and study in a yeshiva. In learning, I found the source of my light. I first started subduing my rebellious spirit to God's law. This required a trust I had barely begun to cultivate. I first tasted humility when I realized I lived in a spinning universe and could no longer tolerate it. Revelation fixed a meaning to life. For the first time ever I rejoiced in the fulfillment of a purpose."

Sometimes, we come to know God through other people. Try to be more aware of others. Listen carefully. God often speaks through those who seem least likely to be holy messengers.

Don't expect everything to happen at once. The contemporary talmudist Adin Steinsaltz once said, "Expecting too much of yourself is one way to keep yourself from doing anything."

Expecting too much to happen too quickly also is a good way of blinding yourself to what actually is happening. Trees that look dormant, even dead, in winter are really preparing themselves for rebirth in spring.

Have a sense of your goal. Then, do your best to keep heading in the right direction—toward Step Four. Don't expect to get there without being aware of the journey that carried you forward, with all its hardships and wonder.

HELP FROM OUR TRADITION

At first, Adam apparently thought he was responsible for everything. Such a big burden for a person who had just been created. When the sun set on the first evening after Adam's creation, he exclaimed, "Woe is me! Because I have sinned, the world has become dark all about me; it will surely return to chaos! With this death, Heaven is punishing me!" All night he sat, fasted and wept; Eve did the same. Just as dawn was about to break, Adam said, "This is just the way things are." And he arose...

Babylonian Talmud,
Avodah Zarah 5a

Prayer and communication with God takes many forms and shapes, including silence. The rabbinic interpretation called *midrash* emphasizes the powerful aspect of silence when contemplating God.

When God revealed Torah, no bird sang or flew, no ox bellowed, the angels did not fly, the Seraphim (ministering angels) ceased from saying, " *Kadosh, Kadosh, Kadosh* (Holy, Holy, Holy)," the sea was calm, no creature spoke; the world was silent and still, and the divine voice said: "I am Adonai your God..." If you are surprised at this, think of Elijah: when he came to Mount Carmel, and summoned all of the priests of Baal, and said to them, "Cry aloud, for He is God," God caused all the world to be still, and those above and those below were silent, and the world was, as it were, empty and void, as if no creature existed, as it says, "There was no voice nor any answer" (1 Kings 18:27, 29). For if anyone had spoken, the priests would have said: "Baal has answered us." So, at Sinai, God made the whole world silent, so that all the creatures should know that there is no god beside God and so God spoke: "I am Adonai your God," and so too in the days to come, God will say, "I, I alone, am the One who comforts you." (Isaiah 51:12)

Exodus Rabbah, Yitro 29:90

Jews throughout history have tried to figure out how to live the way God wants them to live. The words of Bachya ibn Pakuda, a

Spanish Jew who lived in the eleventh century, may help. In his book *Duties of the Heart,* he wrote something that may direct your thoughts heavenward, help you make that decision you want to make, and move you forward to the next step:

"You know best what is for my good. If I articulate my desires, it is not to remind You, but so that I might better understand how greatly dependent I am on You. If then, afterwards, I ask You for things that are not in my best interest, it is because I am humbly ignorant. I acknowledge that Your choice is better than mine and I give myself over to You and the Divine direction of my life."

SOMETHING TO THINK ABOUT

The one who takes on the yoke of God's will is freed from the yoke of worldly concerns, but the one who throws off the yoke of God's will is burdened with the yoke of worldly concerns.

Pirke Avot 3:5

Make God's will your will so that God makes your will the Divine will. Let not your will take precedence over God's will so that God does not make the will of others the Divine will in place of yours.

A MEDITATION

Strive to do the will of God with a perfect heart and a willing soul. Efface your will even if the will of God seems like a burden for you.

Mahzor Vitry

A PRAYER

Each day God gives us the potential to begin again, as if reborn. As a reminder, we are thus prepared to start each day with: *Modeh ani lifanecha, melech chai v'kayam, shehechazarta bi nishmati v'chemla raba emunatecha.* In translation: I stand before You, God with humble thanks. You who empower me with every breath that I take, You, who have faith in me, have returned my life to me, and I will be forever grateful.

CONTEMPORARY VOICES FOR RECOVERY

Love itself is an act of faith. Our mistake is to believe that it is an act of faith in the beloved. Surely faith in the beloved is part of it, but deeper is faith in the world, in the presiding Spirit of the world. When we love, we have faith that this universe will be kind to love, believes in it with us, will enable it to grow. Through faith, love is granted its measure of immortality. Fragile creatures cling to one another. We are buffeted by misfortune. Faith crosses the bridge of longing, the gulf of loss....

Love is one of the ways we grope toward God. Amid all our doubts and wonderment, there is another person in the world whose spirit catches our own. Her eyes sparkle, and something makes us feel suddenly alive, alive on a more vivid plane than we were a moment before. The change is in us and in the world. The marvels we have heard of now live in us. The rudderless world suddenly seems fashioned by a Spirit whose hand is that of an artist. Love has lent us faith.

Rabbi David Wolpe[7]

REFLECTIONS

M. GRINBERG
THE DUNG GATE
"MENTIONED IN THE BOOK OF
NEHEMIAH"

STEP FOUR

COURAGE

Made a searching and fearless moral inventory of ourselves.

- You must constantly struggle to know yourself.
- The only way we can get at the essence of our problem is through deep inner searching. It's the only way to find the truth.
- This searching reveals things we may never have thought possible.
- Make a mental checklist. Search the surface. Then probe more deeply until you have approached the very essence of who you really are or what you have become.

For some, step four is terrifying and painful. Don't try this step prematurely. Use the confidence you have developed during the first three steps to sustain your work on Step Four.

The mere thought of self-examination makes us want to put up our defenses. We want to protect ourselves. Who among us wants to be exposed to the world? Searching ourselves takes great courage.

Be honest and open with yourself. Acknowledge what you have found, and move forward. But remember: only you know what you have found. You will have to do something about it—but you don't have to tell others until you are ready.

Listen to what this man told us: "As far as I was concerned, Purim (the carnival-like Feast of Lots) was amateur night. But it provided another excuse, another rationalization. ' *L'chaim* (For Life),' I would say, but I knew deep down that I meant just the opposite."

Take it slow. You'll get where you are going. You may be tempted to compare yourself with others—to make you feel better or to increase your pain, thinking it will somehow help. Resist this temptation. Focus on your own healing.

Take a deep breath and dig in. It's never easy to go on a faultfinding mission when you are its target. We are taught in *Tur Orach Chayim,* a Jewish legal code prepared by Yaakov ben Asher:

> Pious ones of old used to meditate and concentrate in prayer until they rid themselves of the physical. They nurtured a spiritual strength that bordered on the level of prophecy.

Try it. Choose a favorite line of sacred text and concentrate on it. Repeat it over and over until it sings like a song on your lips. Make it your own. Some possibilities:

- "In all your ways, acknowledge God." (Proverbs 3:6)
- "Wherever you go, God goes with you." (Deuteronomy Rabbah 2:10)
- "Serve God with reverence, tremble as you rejoice." (Psalm 2:11)
- "Keep me, O God, for I have found refuge in You." (Psalm 16:1)

Now, the job will be a little easier—not because there will be less to find, but because you are stronger for having done it this way. In Judaism, this is called a *cheshbon hanefesh,* literally, an accounting of the soul.

Self-examination is an important part of Jewish tradition. We set aside time each Jewish year, at the beginning and at the end, for self-reflection, for making amends.

What did you find? There are many good things to help you get back on your feet. Start with them. In *Avot de Rabbi Natan,* a kind of academy discussion based on *Pirke Avot* (a talmudic tractate containing the rabbis' everyday wisdom), it is written: "The eye is shown only what it is capable of seeing, and the ear hears only what it is capable of listening to."

It will take some time to find out what you need to know. You probably will have to look again and again—perhaps for several days on end. And then repeat the process once more.

Don't forget: all you are trying to find is you. On his deathbed, Rabbi Zusya of Hanipol appeared afraid to face the angel of death. When confronted by his students, he remarked, "I am not afraid that God will ask me why I was not more like Abraham, Isaac, Jacob or even Moses [and we add Sarah, Rebecca, Rachel, Leah, and Zipporah]. I am afraid that God will ask me why I was not more like Zusya."

Zusya's fear also reflects ours. With the deadly support of drink and drugs, we smother our perceptions of inadequacy. We attempt to destroy the person we have decided we can never be or raise ourselves to the person we think we have to be.

Face it: you are who you are. When the drug-induced illusions wear thin, you are left with the same self you began with, somewhat diminished, requiring more chemical support each passing moment. Yet somehow we are never alone. We have the potential to be in an ongoing relationship and dialogue with God, the Holy Blessed One. This is the covenant that God made with the Jewish people, many years ago, atop a fiery mountain called Sinai.

We have to try to live our lives in the constant reflection of that covenant. Like all good relationships, it will not be perfect; at times, it will be strained. Even Moses shattered the first set of commandments. But the midrash tells us that both sets were kept in the Ark of the Covenant as the people traveled to the promised land.

Don't forget the shattered tablets of your life. Keep them next to the new ones that you are carving today. Let them remind you and urge you to go forward to Step Five.

AA, NA, Al-Anon, and other self-help groups can provide you with a fourth-step workbook, a detailed list of questions to answer as part of your fourth-step inventory. They focus on attitudes, responsibilities, self-worth, self-love and love for others, signs of maturity, and an analysis of character traits.

A complement to this: take out the High Holiday prayerbook, the *mahzor,* and turn to the prayers for Yom Kippur. There you will also find questions to ponder, to probe your soul.

It is not a test. You can't pass or fail. These questions are not meant to frighten or discourage you. They are simply there to offer you a renewed life, a life of spiritual renewal.

HELP FROM OUR TRADITION

Rava wrote: If people see that painful sufferings come to them, let them examine their deeds. "Let us search out our way in life and return to Adonai" (Lamentations 3:40). If they examine their deeds and find nothing, let them seek the cause in the neglect of Torah. "Happy is the person whom You instruct, Adonai, and teach from the midst of Torah" (Psalm 94:12). If they still find that this is not the reason, they may be sure these are sufferings of love. "Adonai loves whomever Adonai corrects" (Proverbs 3:12). If the Holy Blessed One loves a person, that person is crushed by God's painful sufferings.

Babylonian Talmud, Berachot 5a

SOMETHING TO THINK ABOUT

Playing this over in our heads helps us; let it guide you through your day, as well. Rebbe Nachman of Breslov taught, "The entire world is a narrow bridge; the main thing is not to be afraid."

TOWARD SOBRIETY, A PSALM

*Be gracious to me, O God
in the measure of your faithfulness
in the measure of your great mercy
erase my transgressions.
Wash me through and through outside
and purify me inside.
Verily I acknowledge my crime
and am ever mindful of my offense.
Against You have I sinned
and done what is evil in Your sight.
Because it is wrong in Your eyes makes it
an*

offense and right in Your judgment.
Indeed You desire truth in the hidden
parts.
Teach me wisdom about secret things.

Psalm 51:3–6, 8

A PRAYER

Praised are You, Adonai, our God, and God of our ancestors. Teach us Your Torah and bring us close to You through *mitzvot.* Lead us away from sin and transgression. Let us not be tempted or disgraced. Let not our impulse to do evil overtake us. Help us to cling to goodness and serve You. Bless us today and every day with loving acts of kindness and mercy in Your sight and in the eyes of all humankind. Praised are You, Adonai, who treats the people Israel with kindness and love.

from the morning liturgy

CONTEMPORARY VOICES FOR RECOVERY

This morning I sat alone, perfectly still in the darkness of an empty sanctuary void of worshipers, of prayer, of music. I listened to the silence, trying to hear the prayers of the many souls that had been there. I wondered, what do they pray when no one is listening? Then, I heard a faint echo. It was like the sound of lives lived in wonder: a choir of sighs and song, of high and low notes, of harmony and dissonance. And in the darkness of the empty sanctuary, I was comforted. I realized that life is not about one painful moment in time. Rather, it is an arc in time. And in that arc, countless souls have prayed and found some small measure of wonder. And despite all the pain, in that small measure of wonder, a light bursts forth.

And in the light—forgiveness.

Rabbi Karyn D. Kedar[8]

REFLECTIONS

M GRINBERG
THE DOUBLE GATE
(ONE OF THE PRINCIPAL ENTRANCE)
THE END OF THE SECOND
TEMPLE PERIOD

STEP FIVE

INTEGRITY

Admitted to God, to ourselves, and to another human being the exact nature of our wrongs.

- When we ask God to listen, we are already reaching out beyond ourselves and entering into a dialogue that will lead to healing.
- Telling God is the easiest. God already knows and forgives.
- Telling ourselves the truth is more difficult.
- Admitting wrongs to another person is the beginning of trust in yourself and in other people.
- When we recall, word for word, what we have done, the healing process will move us forward.

It might seem that it should be easier to approach another human being—even one we have wronged and hurt—before approaching God. When we admit things to God, we feel them in our heart, but they have not yet been translated into our mind. God is always ready to receive us, so we first go to God. When you think the entire world has shut you out, God is always there, ready with ever-supportive, nurturing arms.

The gates of repentance are always open. "Though your sins are scarlet, they shall be white as snow" (Isaiah 1:18). Telling God what we have done wrong may be the easiest admission. Don't expect immediate results. When God listens, that is a blessing in itself.

Even for those accustomed to prayer, approaching God is a humbling experience. The Baal Shem Tov, the founder of Hasidism, has taught us that, through the power of prayer, even the least among us can communicate with God. Every outpouring of the heart, when spoken in earnest and with devotion, is a true prayer. Every hour is an hour of prayer; every modest home and homeless shelter is a house of God. All that is needed is a recognition that we are directed to pray from our inner selves. All that is necessary for prayer is that we pray with passion and sincerity, with hearts full of joy.

It does not happen all at once. According to the rabbis, one of the effects of transgressions is the hardening of the heart. The heart becomes like a rock, solid and impermeable, feeling nothing.

When you begin to admit your wrongs to God, openings develop, like small cracks in a rock. Once your heart begins to open, these cracks begin to widen. Finally, your heart breaks open, and the head begins to know what before only the heart felt.

A friend in recovery told us, "I got clean around Hanukkah time, one day at a time. I remember as we lit the candles each night. It was my own special miracle. I didn't think I could last eight hours without a drug, never mind eight days. Today I'm working on ten years clean, still one day at a time."

Toward the end of Yom Kippur, there is an image that captures the Neilah (final) service. The sun is setting, and we feel as if it is our last chance to confess before God. Then, the *shofar* (ram's horn) is sounded, and the tension that filled our bodies releases in one swift motion. We have made it through another year.

Yom Kippur. It is not just a time to catch up with family and friends, but a spiritual exercise that leaves you spent, like an exhausting physical workout. No pain, no gain.

The alphabet of sins can act as a litany or meditation for you, if you need prompting:

ashamnu, bagadnu, gazalnu, dibarnu dofi, he-evinu, v'hirshanu, zadnu, chamasnu, tafalnu sheker, ya-atznu ra, kizavnu, latznu, maradnu, ni-atznu, sararnu, avinu, pashanu, tzararnu, kishinu oref, rashanu, shichanu, ti-avnu, ta-inu, ti-tanu.

We have trespassed, dealt treacherously, and robbed. We have spoken slander, acted perversely, and wrought wickedness. We have been presumptuous, done violence, and have lied. We have counseled evil, have spoken falsely, and have scoffed. We have revolted, provoked, and rebelled. We have committed iniquity, transgressed, and oppressed. We have been stiff-necked, done wickedly, and corrupted. We have committed abominations, gone astray, and led others astray.

from the Yom Kippur liturgy

The delineation of sins is less important than the flow of words, which takes us heavenward. Just say it: I admit my wrongdoing before You.

We Jews freely interpret God's time frame and willingness to allow people to return. While the Yom Kippur liturgy suggests that we have until the closing prayers of the holiday to repent, some say that individuals have until Hoshanah Rabbah, at the end of Sukkot (the fall harvest festival); others, even until Hanukkah, which falls near the winter solstice, the "darkest day of the year." All this means that basically the opportunity to reach out to God *always* exists.

If we seize this opportunity, God will meet us halfway. That you can count on. The rabbis tell of a king's son who decided to set out on his own. He traveled far from the king's palace before he grew weary, having lost his way. His funds gone, with no place to lodge, he sent word back to the King, who replied: You find the means to begin the journey home, and I will travel to meet you halfway.

But don't just go through the motions, thinking that you can deceive God. Don't withhold details. Some things will be hard to remember. Others will be hard to forget. When you muster the strength necessary to approach God with your misdeeds, then together you and God can face the next task.

Don't worry. If you don't approach God, the Holy Blessed One eventually will call out to you: *AYEKA?*—"Where are you?" Listen hard. This is what God did after Adam had eaten the forbidden fruit. God went looking for Adam. God is waiting for the word *hineini*—"Here am I. I am ready for You."

Thinking that it is a good *mitzvah* (commandment) to eat and drink on the day before Yom Kippur, an unlearned person drank himself into a stupor. He awoke late at night, too late to hear the beckoning tones of Kol Nidrei ("all our vows"—the opening prayer of Yom Kippur). Since he did not know the prayers by memory, he decided to repeat the letters of the Hebrew alphabet over and over, beseeching God to shape them into poetry and the words of prayer.

The following day, he attended the synagogue in Kotzk. After Neilah, the final prayers, the Kotzker rebbe, Menachem Mendl, summoned him. The rabbi queried the man, inquiring about his absence at Kol Nidrei. In the rabbi's presence, he confessed his transgressions, asking whether his manner of reciting the prayers ever could be pardoned. Menachem Mendl responded, "Your prayer was more acceptable than mine. Realizing the error of your ways, you uttered your prayer out of contrition—from the very depths of your being."

We have to learn to face ourselves without being harsh and overly self-critical. When we were critical of ourselves, we could not listen. It got us nowhere.

Remember all the heart-to-hearts you had in front of that early morning mirror? Yet you continued to drink and do drugs, to gamble, to eat excessively. The struggle is constant: you will have to face that mirror every single day of your life. Place it in front of you now. What do you see? Go ahead, say it. If it helps, whisper it or scream aloud. Whatever works for you is OK. Accept whatever you see. Keep doing it until it becomes part of your daily routine.

Rebbe Nachman of Breslov wrote, in his book about ethics and morals called *Sefer Ha-Middot,* that in meditation, people can discuss their inner turmoil with God. Individuals may forgive themselves for actions associated with personal misdeeds, imploring God to grant their fervent prayer to come closer to God. It is impossible to be a good Jew or a good person, taught Rebbe Nachman, without devoting a portion of each day to communing with God in solitude, to having a conversation with Adonai that emanates from the heart.

While you might feel that the requisite concentration is too difficult, try anyway to express your personal thoughts through words. The Breslover Rebbe said: "Words are like water which falls continuously upon a rock until it breaks through."

He concludes by teaching us that in true meditation we cry out to God like a child to a parent who is about to go on a journey. There is no sadness in such weeping—only longing and yearning for return.

Are you ready? Now you have to face the people whom you have wronged. When you speak to another human being, it forces you to speak more clearly and to really hear their reaction.

By speaking to others, we hear ourselves more clearly. Here's where the Jewish tradition really differs from others. God is always there, ready to help—but won't do the work for you. Only you can confront the people whom you have chased away and say simply "I'm sorry," to "beg *mechila*" (ask for forgiveness). Go from person to person. Begin with your neighbor—community starts with two people.

When you admit to someone what you've done, the knowledge that only you know, that's been a heavy burden sapping your strength, is eased because it is now carried by two people instead of just one.

When we admit to ourselves the wrongs we've committed, we may feel ashamed and guilty, isolated and alienated from all humanity. By sharing these wrongs with another person, who can accept us despite our misdeeds and who respects us for our courage in sharing them, we transform these wrongs into a sacred bond, binding us as individuals, neighbors, friends.

HELP FROM OUR TRADITION

The rabbis tell a story about a young boy who could not understand why all this admission stuff was necessary. So the rabbi instructed the child to take a feather pillow and go to the village square, which he did. Next, he was told to rip open the pillow and scatter the feathers throughout the village. Happily, he made quite a mess. Feathers were everywhere. He returned to the rabbi who said to him, "Now go and gather them together—for that is what it is like to try to retrieve all of the words you have misspoken, all of the misdeeds you have done." Understanding, the boy got down on his hands and knees to gather the elusive feathers, which he grasped to his breast, one at a time.

SOMETHING TO THINK ABOUT

Rebbe Nachman said that a human being reaches in three directions: Inward to self, outward to other people, and upward to God. The real secret, taught Nachman, is that the three are one. When we are connected to self, we can reach out to others. When we reach out to others, we may come to know God.

The gates of prayer are sometimes open and sometimes closed, but the gates of repentance are always open. As the sea is always accessible, so is the hand of the Holy Blessed One always open to receive you in penitence.

Deuteronomy Rabbah 2:12

Elimelech of Lizensk taught that a person should tell the teacher who teaches him God's ways, or even a trustworthy friend, all the evil thoughts he has that are in opposition to the holy Torah, which the impulse to do evil brings into his head and heart. He should do so when studying Torah or praying, when lying in bed, or at any other time during the day. He should conceal nothing out of shame.

By speaking these matters, by giving voice to his potential to do evil, he will break the hold of the inclination to do evil so that it will have far less power to entice him on other occasions. All this is apart from the sound spiritual guidance, which is the way of Adonai, that may be received from a teacher or friend. This is a marvelous antidote to the impulse to do evil.

When Israel prays, they do not all pray at once. Rather every congregation prays by itself, first one, then another. After all the congregations finish all the prayers, the angel that oversees prayer takes all the prayers that were said in all the synagogues and makes them into a crown and places them on the head of the Holy Blessed One.

Exodus Rabbah 21:4

TOWARD SOBRIETY, A PSALM

May the presence of Adonai be felt forever.
May Adonai be pleased with the Divine work.
God glances at the earth and it shakes.
God touches the mountains and they tremble.
I will sing to Adonai as long as I live
as long as I exist, I will chant hymns to God.
May my meditation be pleasing to God
that I may go on rejoicing in Adonai.
May sinners disappear from the earth
and the wicked be no more.

Give praise to Adonai. Hallelujah.

Psalm 104:31–35

A PRAYER

May it be Your will, Adonai, our God, to station us in an illumined corner. Let our heart not be sick or our eyes darkened.
Babylonian Talmud, Berachot 17a

CONTEMPORARY VOICES FOR RECOVERY

In quiet, vulnerable moments, we admit to ourselves that we cannot live forever. We will die, leaving the world for those who come after us. Will we have lived well? Will our lives have mattered? Will our successes and sorrows have had meaning? Judaism offers us a chance to say yes. It offers us a chance to join something important, something noble. Something that can tie us to generations of family long ago, and generations we still cannot imagine. It offers us a chance to ask life's most important questions, and to join with other human beings in living our limited days richly, thoughtfully, and enthusiastically, so that at the dusk of life we will be able to look back with satisfaction, with confidence, and even with hope.

Rabbi Daniel Gordis[9]

REFLECTIONS

M. GRÜNBERG
NORTHERN WALL / HEROD'S GATE

A DECORATIVE
DETAIL ADORNING
THE ORIGINAL ENTRANCE
OF THE GATE / THE
SIDE-WALL

STEP SIX

WILLINGNESS

Were entirely ready to have God remove all of these defects of character.

- We pretend to wish away our character defects.
- Working to remove some part of us entirely and leave it with God may help, but that part may never completely go away.
- To reach the point where we are ready to give up any part of self requires great faith.

Every time we think that we have made it, there is more work to do. We were ready to let God do the rest. That would have been easier, but it doesn't work that way. It takes a lot of work to remove some part of us entirely. It may not even be possible. We may have to find ways to live with, and around, it.

Our character defects define us, in a funny kind of way, and protect us at the same time. Thus, we fear that their loss would leave us as a fragment of ourselves, empty and vulnerable.

Gather your courage and strength and make the step work any-how. No person or life is perfect; it only seems that way from far away. When you interact with the world, and with others, something is bound to go wrong. You just have to work harder to set it right.

When the early descendants of Adam corrupted the world, God saw fit to wash it clean. So it is with sobriety. We're at the bottom, wallowing in our own filth. We rely on God to send forth spiritual waters to cleanse us, to wash away the debris we have caused in the depths of our dependency.

Like the generation of the flood, we knew no better. Life was as we thought it should be—because it was as it always had been—or at least as good as we could remember it.

Through the intervention of a Power greater than we previously had conceived, our path toward the good life can be realigned. Our lives have been so corrupted by alcohol and drugs, by overeating and gambling, that we eagerly anticipate the torrential rains that pour down on us. It's like running out into a storm in order to get wet. As painful as these cleansing waters sometimes seem to be, we know deep inside that the rains eventually will clear and we will be restored. The skies seem to have been dark and gloomy forever. But as the sun finally breaks through the clouds, we know that the God upon whom we rely has fulfilled a promise to us. Each time we see a rainbow in the sky, we are reminded of God's promise always to help cleanse us, if we are willing to "come clean." For us Jews, the rainbow becomes a symbol of sobriety, of freedom from overeating and gambling.

God spanned the rainbow across the heavens to color the skies following its most terrible destruction, to serve as an eternal reminder of connection with us. And we recite continually in our hearts:

Baruch ata Adonai, zocher ha-brit.

Praised are You, Adonai [upon whom we rely to] remember this covenant.

The rainbow's sheer beauty can only be experienced in its full brilliance after the darkness of rainstorms. Only now, after plumbing the lowest depths of a dismal existence, do we fully appreciate its beauty.

Jewish mystics teach us that our people had to go down to Egypt and experience slavery before they could taste freedom in Canaan. This person in recovery knows how it feels: "On Yom Kippur, I would sit there with a terrible hangover, a part of me praying that God would let me live another year, a part of me hoping that God would let me die."

According to the rabbis, when a person changes, the old self dies, and a new self is born. Yet, there is an in-between stage when we are neither old nor new self. We step not directly from our old to our new self, but from old self into *nothing.*

This is one reason why so many people need a highly structured treatment program when they first begin recovery. A twelve-step program's structure provides safety and protection when you are new and naked, tender and vulnerable. Like the cocoon that protects the caterpillar during its transformation into a butterfly, the program does not control the changing. Rather, it creates the safe environment in which the new self can be born and nurtured.

What is so frightening about changing is that we find ourselves as someone else without being sure how we became that new person. People in recovery have said to us, "How strange it feels. I like who I am, but it's not really me." To help maintain some continuity in the way we see ourselves is one important reason why Step Six is essential, moving us to Step Seven.

But how do we know that change will happen? Can we be sure that we can count on our God? We're ready, but we're worried. Daily, God purifies our soul. God takes the mess that we offer and reshapes it into its pure form. What we do with it afterwards is up to us.

Here's how Yael I., a friend in recovery, sees it: "Faith to me means giving up the illusion of control I never had. Only my own holiness is in my hands. The disease isolates me and makes me blind. The program has taught me to slow down the panicky blur of my life and reach out to others. Judaism teaches me to trust that I always rest under

God's wing. To be Jewish is to be part of the greater whole, for the promise was given to the nation as a whole. That is worth living for."

HELP FROM OUR TRADITION

Rabbi Alexandri said: "When you leave your things with another human being for safekeeping, even though they might have been new when they were delivered, they often are returned used and worn out. The Holy Blessed One, however, labors differently. When we leave things in God's care, all worn out and tattered, the Holy One returns them to us new. This is so obvious. A worker will work all day and come home exhausted; when asleep, the worker is at peace, since his soul is in the hands of the Holy Blessed One. At dawn, the soul returns newly created for the worker's body. Scripture teaches us, '[Souls] are renewed every morning; great is our dependence on You.'" (Lamentations 3:23)

Tehillim Rabbah 23:7

Although we follow the order as prescribed by the Great Assembly, personal prayer, as it originally existed, is still the most beneficial. Make a habit of praying before God from the depths of your heart, using your own words, in whatever language you know best. Ask God to make you truly worthy of Divine service. This is the essence of prayer.

Rebbe Nachman of Breslov
Likutay Etzot Ha-Shem

SOMETHING TO THINK ABOUT

Once a student said to his teacher, "Rabbi, why is it that God sometimes seems so far away?" The rabbi replied, "Imagine a parent teaching a child to walk. The parent does not hold on to the child. Instead, she holds her arms outstretched away from the child, and the child walks forward in between the arms of her loving parent. As the child comes forward, the parent moves away just a little. How else can the child learn to walk?"

Some say that Psalms are the heart of the Jewish soul. We find that reciting them helps us sleep, soothes us, and moves us forward. Keep a book of Psalms by your bed or on your desk. When you are wrestling with your soul, still looking for reasons to grab that bottle or pop a pill, remember that they can help you climb the heavenly ladder.

TOWARD SOBRIETY, A PSALM

Adonai, hear my voice when I cry out
Take pity on me and answer me.

Do not turn away Your servant in anger
You have been my help.
Never leave me, never desert me
Adonai will care for me still.

Psalm 27:7, 9–10

A PRAYER

Consider reciting these words each morning—or whenever you feel the need for God's purifying waters to wash you clean. Traditionally, the words are part of morning prayers.

My God, the soul which you have given me is pure. You created it. You shaped it into being. And you breathed it into me. Now guard it while it is still in me. One day, you will take it from me, only to return it in the days to come. But as long as my soul still energizes the life that is in me, I will thank you, my God and God of my ancestors, Creator of all life, Divine One of all souls. Praised are You who returns souls to the dead.

CONTEMPORARY VOICES FOR RECOVERY

God is where I come from and where I am going. At any point along this continuum, He alone can know me fully. Knowing me fully, He is able to love me.

What I know of God is that I am created in His image. That is the most profound religious statement I've ever encountered. Not for what it tells me about me, but for what it tells me about God. Since I create the world I live in through language, so must God. Since I can love and nurture, so must God. Since I am easily hurt or destructively angry, so, too, God.

But God's characteristics are not bound by death and, therefore, are fundamentally different from those characteristics in me. There are moments when the qualities we identify as being feminine are essential to my sense of self. Then, God is She, comfortably and lovingly for me.

Rabbi Ira F. Stone[10]

REFLECTIONS

_____

_____

M. GRÜNBERG
JAFFA GATE
— FRONT —

STEP SEVEN

HUMILITY

Humbly asked God to remove our shortcomings.

- Humbly means with acceptance of ourselves with all our limitations. No false arrogance or pride. Our humility brings us in relationship to God.
- You're human. We all are. By definition, we are limited. We carry our limitations with us through life. God helps us grow beyond them.
- Character defects do not simply vanish. With God's help, we can change.

In his step-by-step book about ethics, titled *Mesillat Yesharim,* Moshe Chaim Luzatto taught that among God's loving acts was giving people the opportunity to approach the Divine in the physical world. Although you may be surrounded in darkness, far from the divine light, you can still stand before God and call out the name of the Almighty. This act alone, says Luzatto, elevates you from a lowly state to an incredible level of closeness to God, allowing you to cast your personal burdens on God.

It's tough to be humble, especially when you have lived your life by always being its center. Go ahead: approach God. Feel God's presence in your life. Request what you want. The response may not come back as you anticipated—but listen carefully.

Jews have a difficult time doing this step. Each time we think we "have it," we need to think it through again. The tradition says it best: "Pray as if everything depends on God, but act as if everything depends on you."

We know that we can always depend on God and be received, that we can ask God anything, talk about whatever we want or need. But we also realize way deep down that God does not just remove our shortcomings. Recovery would be a lot easier if that were the case.

Shortcomings have to be worked through, worked around, transcended—all with God's help. But seldom are they fully removed. They remind us that they are still out there, waiting to subvert our good intentions at any time, without warning, if we let them. Don't. Be on your guard. Change your way of living. Draw on the spiritual energy that God has given you, that divine spark.

Seeing our defects clearly, we feel great pain in our hearts. Don't allow those shortcomings to drag you down again and suck you dry. Fight with all you have and God will join you in the struggle. This adult child of alcoholics said it best: "I am still afraid to spin off into pain and drown, all alone. Invisible to myself, I can't imagine what God sees. I don't know why God wants me to be whole."

Look at Moses, God's main agent for over forty years. It's too easy to dismiss him as a storybook hero, larger than life. Yet, he could not even speak right. Still, God chose him to speak to Pharaoh, to lead the Jews out of their slavery and into freedom, to direct their own lives. Moses the stutterer, the stammerer.

Change the name from Moses to that of your AA sponsor, your NA sponsor, your OA sponsor, ACoA sponsor, your Gamblers Anonymous sponsor. Your sponsor, your Moses, may not be very articulate at times, but he/she channels God's holiness for you. Don't ever forget it. Through this person who, like you, fought for—and is still trying to save—their life. Through that person who is trying to save your life, God is joining you in working on your shortcomings. According to Jewish tradition, God will only help you with your shortcomings after you have tried overcoming them yourself. You can always rely on God. But you'll find that with God's special strength in your soul, you will be able to do it yourself and not have to ask God alone to remove your shortcomings.

In his *Sefer Hasidim,* a book of basic concepts on Hasidism, Yehuda He-chasid shows you how to humbly approach God, letting the Holy One suffuse your spirit:

When you pray, do so with a melody that is pleasant and sweet in your own ears. That melody will direct you to pray with a special feeling, since it will lead your heart to follow the direction of your words. When you ask God for something, choose an internal melody that strengthens your heart and when you speak God's praise, choose a song that will make your own heart rejoice. Your mouth will be filled with joyous verses before God who looks directly into your heart. In such a way, you will be able to praise God and come away with overflowing love and happiness.

Don't expect your shortcomings to disappear at once. Don't berate yourself or God when you discover that you've made the same mistake once again.

"Humility." We've heard that word a thousand times, but still can't describe it. Yet it's one of Judaism's primary concepts. How can we not be humbled by God's awesome presence? We Jews cover our heads to constantly remind ourselves that as great as we think we are, there is a much greater Power. We bow the head and bend the knee in prayer to remind ourselves that God is in charge.

It's particularly important to be humble when we ask God to help us remove our shortcomings. Humility is one of the keys that opens the gates of Heaven.

An addict told us, "Before I was in recovery, I was perfect. Now, I'm better." Perfectionism often seems to accompany addiction. Even when we come to see and admit our shortcomings, we expect them to disappear immediately. People who have been sober for years still call themselves recovering alcoholics because they know that although they're better, they're not perfect. And they have to keep choosing between two directions: either recovery or relapse; those are the only choices. It is an ongoing process.

After you've been at your lowest, felt the pain, scraped the bottom of the gutter, you'd think you'd know what it is to be humble. No—not yet. Not until you have picked yourself up and begun to live again can you be humble. Sounds strange, doesn't it?

Try to be humble when you approach God. Work at it. Be straight with God. To be humble is to speak from the strength of your limitations, not to consider yourself dirt or garbage. That is not the Jewish way. Remember, everyone is created in God's image.

HELP FROM OUR TRADITION

Rabbi Bunam of Pzhysha taught: Everyone must have two pockets so that he can reach into one or the other according to his needs. In his right pocket are the words: For my sake the world was created. And in the left: I am dirt and ashes.

Rabbi Joshua ben Levi met Elijah the prophet one day and inquired of him, "When will the Messiah come?"

Elijah responded, "Go and ask him yourself."

"But where is he?"

"He sits at the gates of the town."

"How will I know him?"

"He is sitting among those stricken with leprosy. The others unbind all of their bandages and then rebind them all. But this one unbinds one sore at a time and then rebinds it before attending to the next one. He thinks to himself, 'Perhaps I will be needed today and so I must not delay.'"

Following Elijah's advice, Rabbi Joshua went to the Messiah and spoke to him, "Peace to you, my master and teacher."

"When will you finally come?" Rabbi Joshua asked. "Today," came the quick reply.

When Joshua returned to Elijah, the prophet asked, "Well, what did he say?"

"He lied to me," said Joshua, "He told me that he would come today but he has not come."

Elijah gently responded, "You misunderstood. He told you: 'Today—if you will only hearken to God's voice.'" (Psalm 95:7)

Babylonian Talmud, Sanhedrin 98a

SOMETHING TO THINK ABOUT

To an earthly monarch one goes with arms overflowing with gifts and returns empty handed. To God, one goes with empty hands and returns with a full spirit.

Pesikta Rabbati

Rabbi Yochanan and Rabbi Elazar both said, "Even if a sword is on your neck, do not refrain from praying for mercy."

Babylonian Talmud, Berachot 10a

TOWARD SOBRIETY, A PSALM

Remember Your compassion and mercy, Adonai,
for they have existed since ages past.
Do not remember the sins of my youth and
wrongdoing but remember me in love for the
sake of your righteousness, Adonai.
Good and upright is Adonai, therefore God shows the way to sinners.
You guide the humble to justice.
You teach the humble Your way.

Psalm 25:6–9

A PRAYER

You reach out Your hand to uplift
You extend Your welcome to those
returning in teshuvah
It is You who taught us to confess all
wrongs before You
That we might stop hurting other people
That we might be welcomed in Your
presence.

Ata Noteyn Yad
from the High Holiday Mahzor

CONTEMPORARY VOICES FOR RECOVERY

The life of spirit ebbs and flows. There are times in our lives when we are open to religious experience, when we are ripe to find connection, meaning, in every stream of sunlight, in the sight of winter birds coming into formation, catching a glimpse of a now-grown daughter asleep, your eyes suddenly able to peel back the years of a child's face underneath. A hundred possibilities in nature and in human meeting. Every few days we seem to have another encounter with some new person in which we feel what is holy passing between us. Maybe those are the experiences we call Sinai.

Merle Feld[11]

REFLECTIONS

_____

_____

M. GRIMSKY (GATES OF HULDA) JERUSALEM.

STEP EIGHT

LOVE

Made a list of all persons we had harmed, and became willing to make amends to them all.

• You make the list because you are accepting responsibility for the consequences of your behavior, without regard to why you did what you did or what caused you to do it.

• There may be many people you harmed, intentionally or unintentionally. We often harm those we love most and wish to harm least. Begin with them.

• Express a willingness to say that you are responsible. Say it aloud.

• Rehearse in your mind and in your heart how you will do whatever you can do to undo whatever you did—and anticipate the relief that will follow.

For some people, making a list sounds silly. "Why do I need a list? I know all too well whom I've hurt." A list may be too painful to write down. "It will constantly remind me of what I've done and whom I've hurt." That's the point.

Memory is central to being a Jew. Once you make a list of everyone you have hurt, you will know what you still have to do.

Lists imply order, which we constantly are trying to bring back into our lives. Some people think that there is too much order in Judaism, too many details for doing almost everything. But we Jews believe that if we follow a specific way of doing things, an order that has worked for so many for so long, we have a better chance of reaching our goal: recovery, closeness to God. Closeness to our family, friends, and self. What else could we ask for?

As Jews, we are taught that part of our task is to restore order and goodness to the world. We have a powerful compulsion to mend the world's imperfections, to make it more fair, to correct injustice, to right what is wrong. Too often, we focus on correcting other people's wrongdoings, such as fighting the injustices they've caused.

The Eighth Step prepares us to begin making the world a better place by correcting the injustice that has come from what we have or haven't done.

As Jews, there are specific times during the year when we specifically consider whom we've wronged. But don't wait until Yom Kippur. Make your list now.

Taking direction from the Yom Kippur liturgy, ask yourself: Who are the people I have hurt by doing something to them? Or by not doing something? Whom did I harm by telling tales about them? Whom did I insult or jeer? Whom did I mislead or neglect? Towards whom was I unkind? Whom did I hurt by yielding to my addiction? To whom did I cause pain by robbing or stealing? Who was hurt by my weakness or violence?

Make your list. Next, figure out how you can begin to make up for the pain you caused. This is not moral algebra. The list may raise old resentments, hurts, angers. Don't try to crack the entire nut at once. Begin slowly.

There are some people you may have harmed out of thoughtlessness or inconsideration. They did nothing to offend or harm you. You want to make it better. This is not a bad place to begin.

You may not be ready to make amends to everyone. That's OK. For some people on your list, now is not the time to act. Just think. That's hard enough right now. When the time comes to make amends, God will provide opportunities to do so. But that can wait until you are ready for the next step.

With some people, our feelings about making amends may be hesitant, even resentful. We may still be hurt and angry and that anger may eat away at us. We'd rather rot than make amends to them!

Begin where you are, where you can. These twelve steps are a process, to be worked through again and again, each time going a little deeper into your soul. Next time, go a little farther; be willing to do a little more. Don't get stuck here because you can't yet make amends with everyone. Let the humility of Step Seven make you realize that you can't do it all and at once—but take strength and begin.

HELP FROM OUR TRADITION

Rabbi Abraham Isaac Kook wrote, "My hope is that God, in His mercy, will grant me a complete healing among the other sick persons of His people Israel, and that in His abundant kindness He will enable me to return to Him in love. Especially do I pray that He enable me to mend whatever wrong I may have committed, whether in man's relationship to God or man's relationship to man, and that He grace me with the opportunity to repay my debts.

"To my great regret I do not remember all my debts in detail. But I hope that God will bestir me and remind me of them all, and that He will help me to repay them."

SOMETHING TO THINK ABOUT

One must never say to one who has repented and changed his way of life, "Remember your former transgressions."

Babylonian Talmud, Baba Metzia 58b

TOWARD SOBRIETY, A PSALM

I became Your charge at birth
from my mother's womb
You have been my God.
Do not keep your distance
for trouble is pressing and
there is none to help but You.
Many bulls surround me
mighty bulls of Bashan encircle me.
They open their mouths at me
like tearing, roaring lions.
My vitality is poured out
all my bones are separated.
My heart is like wax
melting within me.
My strength is dried up like a shard
My tongue sticks to my palate
You commit me to the dust of death
But You, Adonai, don't keep your distance,
my strength, speed to my help.
Save my life from the sword, my precious
life from the clutches of a cur.
Deliver me from the lion's mouth, from
the horns of wild oxen, respond to me.

Psalm 22:11–17, 20–22

A PRAYER

My God, keep my tongue from causing harm and my lips from telling lies about people. Let me keep silent if people curse me. Let my soul remain humble and at peace. Open my heart to Your teaching; give me the will to practice it. May the scheming plans of those who seek my harm come to naught. *Yihyu l'ratzon imrei fi v'hegyonlibi lifanecha, Adonai Tzuri v'Goali.* May the words of my mouth and the meditations of my heart be acceptable to You, Adonai, my Rock and Redeemer.

from the end of the Amidah prayer
(the core prayer of Jewish worship, said
standing)

CONTEMPORARY VOICES FOR RECOVERY

In every worldly sensation, there is an element of infinite love. This love is unconditional yet not exclusive. The one love you yearn for most is unconditional love. The one love that is hardest to give is unconditional love. True love is free from expectations and empty of preconceived notions. In unconditional love there are no disappointments, for there are no expectations; there are no rejections, for there are no preconceived notions. Unconditional love is giving yourself fully and receiving fully. In letting go of your own agenda and expanding the possibilities for receiving and giving love, you are able to surpass stubborn obstacles and emerge through the narrow confinements of your perception to greater visions of holiness and goodness.

Rabbi Shoni Labowitz[12]

REFLECTIONS

M. GRINBERG / DAMASCUS GATE / JERUSALEM.

STEP NINE

DISCIPLINE

Made direct amends to such people whenever possible, except when to do so would injure them or others.

• Do it. Don't just talk or think about it. It's OK to begin with the easy ones. Just do it.

• Do it face-to-face if possible and appropriate. Don't have the conversation with yourself. Don't have a conversation just in your head.

• Some things that we do have consequences that cannot be undone. There are also things we cannot yet bring ourselves to do. But, if you can't fix whatever it is, go fix something else.

• Move forward in recovery and do whatever you can do to transform the pain into peace. Experience the release. But be careful not to become someone whose apology gives personal release while causing more pain.

"There is a time to act," says Ecclesiastes. Now is the time. For us Jews, the deed is more important than the thought; who we are is equal to what we do. Not what we think or say we will do. Wonderful thoughts do not repair the world; small deeds begin to do so.

Making amends may be difficult. The first time may be terrifying. But going to someone and simply saying, "I'm sorry" gets easier each time you do it. So get out and go do it. Be ready to listen to someone tell you how hurt they are and how angry they were. Just ask them what you can do to try to make things right.

Of course, you're afraid to do it. Just as denying your addiction did not make it go away—it simply let you pretend that things were fine and made you feel continually worse—so your failure to make amends magnifies your sense of emptiness, imperfection, being fatally flawed.

You had to face the pain of addiction to begin on the road to recovery, and you had to share the Fourth Step inventory with someone else before beginning to correct your character defects. So now you must seek forgiveness from those you have harmed before beginning the task of rebuilding your world.

Go out and do what you have to do. But, be careful. Don't add insult to injury by trying to repair something for your sake—rather than for the sake of the person you hurt. Whatever you do, do it *l'shem shamayim,* for the sake of heaven.

Sometimes, the process will be surprisingly easy. You simply apologize and the other person is so relieved to see that you have changed, they just accept your apology. Others will not be so forgiving. Don't let them renew your anger or your guilt. Take charge of the process.

But you are not responsible for the results. Making amends to some people may, in a peculiar way, cause more pain by opening up healed wounds. Talk about this dilemma with a trusted friend or your sponsor.

Amends can also be made indirectly. If you have stolen, repay your debt or return it anonymously. Or give *tzedakah* (a charitable donation) as amends for people from whom you have stolen whom you can't find or never knew.

Making such amends simultaneously heals ourselves and the world. By fully participating in personal recovery, we begin to actively restore *shalom,* unity and wholeness, to the world.

HELP FROM OUR TRADITION

If your deeds exceed your good intentions, your good intentions endure. But if your good intentions are more plentiful than your good acts, then your good intentions do not endure.

Pirke Avot 3:9

They asked wisdom, what shall be the punishment of the sinner? Wisdom answered: Evil pursues sinners (Proverbs 13:21). They asked prophecy. It replied: The soul that sins will die (Ezekiel 18:4). They asked Torah. It replied: Let him bring a sacrifice (Leviticus 1:4). But then they asked God and God replied: Repent and obtain atonement, My children. What do I ask of you? Only to seek Me and live.

Pesikta d'Rav Kahana 24:7

SOMETHING TO THINK ABOUT

Repentance makes an individual a new creature. Previously a person may be dead through sin, now he is fashioned afresh.

Psalms Rabbah

TOWARD SOBRIETY, A PSALM

Adonai is my shepherd
I lack nothing
God gives me my ease in rich pastures,
Leads me to take my drink by tranquil waters
Redeems my life
Leads me in the ways of right.

Out of sheer graciousness
Though I go through the gloomiest valleys
I fear no misfortune for You are ever with
me,
Your sustaining staff is what relieves me
of my anxiety.
My enemies do not bother me because You
are watching over me.
You have made my heart fat with richness,
my cup runs over.
As long as I live my tracks will be
accompanied by graciousness.
I will dwell in Adonai's house as long as I
live.

Psalm 23

A PRAYER

Before a person is healed, he must
acknowledge his illness.
Before a person finds light, she must know
her own darkness.
Before a people is forgiven, it must confess
its sins.
We confess our sins and those of our
fellows for we are responsible, one for the
other.

90

Heal us, Adonai, and lead us through darkness to light.

from the Yom Kippur confessional

CONTEMPORARY VOICES FOR RECOVERY

The past is past. We can look at it one way or we can look at it some other way, but in the end it is what it is, and the energy we spend on stirring it up could better be used to deal constructively with the present.

Not having to fix the past is liberating. Rather than having to channel our energy into undoing past wrongs, we can focus on doing what is right in the present. Doing what is right may mean seeking to make amends for past wrongs, but even this cannot erase those wrongs. We have to accept the past, learn from it, and eventually let it go so that we can make what we can of the present.

Rabbi Rami Shapiro[13]

REFLECTIONS

M. GRÜNBERG / SINGLE GATE / JERUSALEM

STEP TEN

PERSEVERANCE

Continued to take personal inventory and when we were wrong promptly admitted it.

• Take pride that you are continuing, not beginning. Recovery is a process. Ongoing. It never stops.

• Build a habit of self-reflection in approaching everything that you do.

• You will slip and fall, but as soon as you realize you have done wrong, be quick to admit it. Don't wait for others to point a finger.

Once you have started, don't stop. Recovery is like breathing. If you want to stay alive, you have to do it. Go easy. Establish a rhythm that works for you. You may want to begin at night to prepare yourself for the next day. Or take periodic reviews during the day. Some even find it helpful to do a "reality check" once an hour, on the hour.

In Judaism, there is a tradition to arise early to do a *mitzvah.* Make it right early in the morning. As a result, your entire day will be more tranquil.

Use the rhythm of the Jewish day—three times of prayer—to stop and review your behavior. Cease your usual activities. Step out of yourself and look at things the way God might look at them. Use Shabbat to review your week, to take a step back and see how far you've come (not just how much farther you have to go). Measure your time by the sacred signposts of our tradition: rituals, festivals, holidays.

However you decide to do it, set aside time each day and each week to review what you have done and what you have said. (We call these "Sabbath moments," time to pause, reflect, and gain strength to move forward in recovery.) But don't wait for Shabbat to make amends for when you have erred and temporarily have lost your footing. As soon as you realize that you are wrong, admit it. Stop everything. Step back and look at yourself objectively. Bachya ibn Pakuda taught that "Days are scrolls. Write on them what you want remembered."

Prior to the High Holidays, we take inventory and make amends. But once a year is not enough. The goal is to be able to step back from everything we do and look at ourselves objectively. Few among us can really do that. We find it helpful to develop a regular routine for taking our personal inventory.

As Jews, we pray for the messianic era, but realize that, until it arrives, our task is to make the world a place ready for Messiah. Actually, Shabbat provides us with a window into the messianic era. We all long for that time when peace and tranquility will pervade the world, and so we work all week to get a glimpse of it for such a short time.

The process of recovery is lifelong—we can't say that enough. As Jews, we are expected to take inventory and make amends. The Jewish tradition teaches that we are not required to finish the work, but neither are we free to desist from it. But we are not just Jews. We are addicted Jews who slip easily into denial; into a certain blindness, grandiosity, or perfectionism; into a failure to listen carefully enough to what others say.

That's why this step instructs us to take inventory again, even though we did it once in Step Four, to establish a continuous process. But Step Ten is different from Step Four. There we just took a moral inventory. Here we monitor our recovery. The inventory and the action to correct any wrongdoing becomes one and the same, simultaneous. One can no longer exist without the other. One friend told us, "Recovery did not prevent me from making mistakes. It made me recognize them sooner after I had made them."

HELP FROM OUR TRADITION

When good people give up their integrity to do what is wrong, they die; in doing that wrong, they die. When evil people turn away from this death to do what is right and just, they actually save their lives. When they recognize all their sins and turn away from those sins, they live and do not die. Yet, the house of Israel objects: The way of Adonai is unjust. "Is it My ways that are unjust, O house of Israel? I will judge each one of you by what you do," says Adonai. "Return and turn away from all your sins, or your iniquity will be your downfall. Throw off all the burdens of past sins. Make yourself a new heart and a new spirit. House of Israel, why should you die? I take no pleasure in the death of anyone," says Adonai. "Just repent and live."

Ezekiel 18:26–32

SOMETHING TO THINK ABOUT

It is not your responsibility to fully complete the work of repair, but neither are you free to cease from doing it.

Pirke Avot 2:16

TOWARD SOBRIETY, A PSALM

Search me, God, and know my heart
Test me and know my thoughts
See if the path to despair is yet within me
and lead me in the path of eternity.

Psalm 137:23–24

A PRAYER

Listen, Adonai, for I am in distress. My spirits are troubled. My heart is turned within me, for I have grievously rebelled. In the street the sword is bereft, in the house it is like death. May you bring the day (of my return) ... for my sighs are many and my heart faint.
Lamentations 1:20–22

CONTEMPORARY VOICES FOR RECOVERY

When we do something wrong, because we are human and our choices are so complicated and temptations so strong, we don't lose our humanity. But we lose our integrity, our sense of wholeness, of being the same person all the time. We create a situation where a part of us, our good self, is at war with another part of us, our weak and selfish side. We lose the focus, the singleness of purpose, that enables us to do the things that matter to us. That is when we need the religious gift of forgiveness and atonement (making our split selves *at one*). But should we ever conclude that there is no point in trying to be good because we can never be good enough, that is when we lose everything. Being human can never mean being perfect, but it should always mean struggling to be as good as we can and never letting our failures be a reason for giving up the struggle.

Rabbi Harold Kushner[14]

REFLECTIONS

M. Grinberg
THE NEW GATE
JERUSALAM
WEST SIDE

STEP ELEVEN

ILLUMINATION

Sought through prayer and meditation to improve our conscious contact with God as we understand God, praying only for God's will for us and the power to carry that out.

- Don't wait for inspiration; look for it. You are the seeker. It's still up to you.
- Use whatever means you can to make a contact with God. Make a commitment to pray, meditate, and talk in your own special voice.
- Doing it is much more important than how you do it.
- Once you have allowed God to enter into your life, build a relationship of understanding.
- Seek to understand the dimensions of your relationship with God and of God's relationship with you.
- Pray for inspiration and the strength to do what you have to do.

Judaism teaches that we can come into contact with God through any activity done with the right intent—repairing shoes, weeding a garden, waxing the car, even paying our taxes! Since God is present in all things and all people, we can come into conscious contact with God through any of our interactions with the world. Through these interactions, we become aware of God's presence in our lives. One of the best ways of coming into contact with God is through prayer and meditation.

Communication with the Divine is possible through many types of expression. For most of us, who are not great speakers, we rely on others' poetry to reach out to God. Joseph Albo, in *Sefer Ha-Ikkarim,* taught:

> In prayer, you gather the strength of dedication for life, allowing this life to become the fulfillment of the Divine will, the furthering of Holy purpose—a contribution to the success of that purpose, which God has established for all humanity and for the people Israel. Thus, the flavor of all prayer is the resolution which infuses the entire person and unites all of you to serve God through living.

Call together all your powers of concentration. Remove all distracting thoughts from your mind so that, when you pray, your thoughts are focused. Were you speaking to an earthly monarch, you would be extremely careful with your words, painstakingly choosing each one, so as not to say anything wrong. When you pray, you are speaking before the Holy Blessed One. Therefore, concentrate even more; God probes all thought. Before God, thought is the same as speech.

Both prayer and meditation are ways of coming into contact with God, of getting in touch with the Divine will. In some ways, these two approaches correspond to two different ideas about God. Mystics generally see God beyond the limits of our physical world. They direct their prayers and thoughts outward. Others see God as deeply within us, in that place where our will commingles with God's will. They see prayer and meditation focused inward, helping us to look deeper into ourselves.

Jewish meditation is very simple. Set aside time each day to talk with God. We find it helpful to speak out loud in a quiet voice, in a quiet place and in solitude. Some people have a special area where they most easily come into contact with God. Try different ways and places until you find your own. Treasure it and use it.

Just as it is important to call your sponsor when you don't need help, so that you can call her when you do, make contact with God when everything seems fine. If you do, in those troubled times when you feel most alone, you will know that God still is there, ever ready to listen.

Listen to the words of someone involved in the struggle to keep sober:

I am one of God's people, and one who has been chosen to find recovery. Thanks to the Twelve Step path I have begun to understand God's will for me, and never again can I claim ignorance of my actions. Yes, I will stray from the path from time to time. I am an imperfect creature of body and spirit. Nevertheless, God's will for me is simple: Just do the right thing.

As a Jew, I believe that God asks only one thing from me. God asks that I show my love; and God gives me opportunities to prove that love.

HELP FROM OUR TRADITION

Where does God dwell? This was the question with which the rabbi of Kotzk surprised a number of learned students who happened to be visiting him. They laughed, "What a thing to ask. Is it not written, 'The whole world is a manifestation of God's glory'?" Then the rabbi answered his own question: "God dwells wherever people allow the holy to fill their lives."

The Maggid of Meziritch taught in his book on mysticism *Esser Orot,* "When one studies and prays with fear and love, that individual gains much from it. He becomes bound in his thoughts to the Creator, blessed be God. Such a worshipper sees nothing and hears nothing except the divine vitality that is in all things.

For everything is from God; it is only clothed in different garments."

A MEDITATION FOR TIMES OF WEARINESS AND DESPAIR

The people of Israel say, "We are poor. We have no sacrifices to bring as an offer." God replies, "I need only your words, as it is written, 'Take with you words [of Torah]'" (Hosea 25:2). God replied, "Weep and pray, and I will receive you."

Shemot Rabbah 38:4

TOWARD SOBRIETY, A PSALM

Listen to my words, Adonai,
Consider my inmost thoughts
My Sovereign God, hear my voice
To You alone do I pray
Adonai, hear my morning prayers
I lay them before You
in anxious anticipation.

Psalm 5:1–4

A PRAYER FROM SOMEONE IN RECOVERY

Blessed art Thou, O Lord,
every day,
Because every day is precious,
Every day is a lifetime
mirroring all life itself.
Thank you for the morning
when I feel fresh and young
And wake to the beauty
all around me.
Thank you for the afternoon
when the sun is high
Suspended in triumph
above a work-a-day world.
Thank you for the evening when
the shadows cast a sheltering
palm above the universe
Permitting it to pause
ready for the dark.
Thank you for the night
with the ever-present stars
To remind me that darkness
is never absolute.
Thank you for the calm
that is restorative,
Not a mindless obliteration
of reality.
Thank you for the sleep

that heals and strengthens
And fills my heart with hope
for a new tomorrow.

Marcia H.

CONTEMPORARY VOICES FOR RECOVERY

In God's desire to see if he [Abraham], like each of us in our own way, can survive in a world which lacks guarantees, the Divine called to Abraham from the heavens. Upon hearing God's call, Abraham responded with the word *hineini,* affirming his willingness to do whatever God would ask of him. Abraham did not wait for God to spell out the task nor did he ask for any guarantees. This is exactly what the term *hineini* signifies—being ready to respond within the context of relationship, regardless of the nature of the request. *Hineini* can teach us about the very essence of relationship; about our relationships, not only with God but with other human beings.

Rabbi Norman Cohen[15]

REFLECTIONS

M. Grinberg / THE GOLDEN GATE / JERUSALEM

STEP TWELVE

SERVICE

Having had a spiritual awakening as a result of these Steps, we tried to carry this message to alcoholics and to practice these principles in all of our affairs.

• Once you've had a spiritual awakening, it's yours forever. It may not feel near all the time, but it's never very far away. You have to reach for it.

• Being alive physically is no longer enough. There is so much more to life. Acknowledge your rebirth and renewal by living life fully.

• Share the message. Help others find the path to recovering that these steps gave to you. Preaching is good. So is teaching. But teaching and preaching by working the program is best of all.

• Let these insights influence all that you do.

• This spiritual awakening will affect your work, play, eating, sleeping, and many other activities that you do not think of as spiritual.

• Carry the message to anyone who is in need and needs to listen: alcoholics, addicts, overeaters, gamblers, codependents, and everyone else.

You have reached the final step in your recovery—an awesome experience. Now these steps have become part of your everyday routine; they are now part of you. You are unable to distinguish where the steps end and you begin. More than that, your Judaism has been renewed through these steps. Work them again and again. Just as each Passover we are back in Egypt again as slaves, so each time we rework a step, we confront our addiction anew.

Now take what you have learned and reach out to someone else in need. It's the only way to go further. It helps both of you. And remember the further forward you go, the further from your addiction you'll be. This friend in recovery said to her sponsor, "How can I ever thank you?" The reply, "Just carry the message, carry the message."

Yet, it's important to concentrate on your own practice of the Twelve Steps before you carry its message to others. Teaching and practice. Our rabbis said:

> Regarding the person who learns in order to teach, Heaven will allow that person to continue to learn and to teach. But concerning the one who learns in order to practice, Heaven allows that person to learn and teach, observe and practice.

Pirke Avot 4:5

Practicing these principles—honesty, taking responsibility for our actions, making amends when appropriate, and promptly admitting to others when we are wrong—helps us maintain our sobriety and carry the message to others in the most powerful way possible: through personal example.

At first, you may be shy when it comes to talking about your recovery or your relationship to God through Judaism. It takes time. But it's important to talk about the Twelve Steps in the context of Torah. Listen to the words of our tradition:

> "If three have eaten at the same table and have not spoken words of Torah, it's as if they had made sacrifices to dead idols." God's will is not in their thoughts. "But if three have eaten at the same table and the words of Torah were spoken, it's as if they had eaten at the table of Adonai." (Pirke Avot 3:3)

As a reentry point in Judaism, as a vehicle to *mitzvot* (divine commandments), let these words of our tradition begin to inform all of what you say, what you do, and how you live. We have accepted the mission to be "a light to the nations." Now go and bring others on the journey with you.

HELP FROM OUR TRADITION

How did Zusya bring a person to repentance? He went down all of the steps until he reached the other person's level. Then Zusya bound the roots of his soul to the roots of the other person, and together their souls did repentance.

SOMETHING TO THINK ABOUT

Said the Leover Rebbe: If someone comes to you for assistance and all you say to him is "God will help you," you become a disloyal servant of God. It is for you to understand that God has sent you to aid the needy and not to refer him back to God.

One who prays for merely his own needs is like one who works to strengthen his home alone, and does not want to help the people of his land strengthen the walls of the city. Even though he expends much effort, he remains in danger. But one who includes himself with the community expends little and remains safe.

Yehuda Halevi
The Kuzari

The difference between one who prays and one who does not pray is not to be found in the fact that the former sets aside time everyday for his prayer, while the latter does not. There is a more basic dichotomy. The types of lives those two people live are thoroughly different. The time devoted to prayer makes an impression upon every aspect of the entire day.

Abraham Isaac Kook
Olat Reiyah

A number of unbelievers lived in Rabbi Meir's neighborhood. This used to really bother him. He was so annoyed that he wanted to pray for them to die. Meir's wife, Beruriah, advised him, "Do not pray for an end to sinners, but an end to sin. Pray that they repent."

Babylonian Talmud, Berachot 10a

TOWARD SOBRIETY, A PSALM

Out of the depths of despair I called
to You, Adonai,
Adonai, hear my voice.
Let Your ears respond to my pleading
Adonai, if You should keep track of sins
Adonai, who could stand?
But with You there is forgiveness,
For this You are held in awe.
I hope in Adonai

My soul has hope
and for Your word I wait.
My soul waits for Adonai
More than watchmen for the morning
Waiting for the sunrise
Israel, hope is in Adonai
for which Adonai is continuous love
and Your great redeeming Power
It is You who redeems Israel
from all their sins.

Psalm 130

A PRAYER

Praised are You, Adonai our God, Sovereign of the Universe, who makes a distinction between holy and profane, between light and darkness, between Israel and the nations, between the Sabbath and the six working days. Praised are You, Adonai, who makes a distinction between holy and profane.

from the Havdalah liturgy,
which separates Sabbath and the
holidays from the rest of the calendar

The conclusion of true *teshuvah,* returning to our Source in Heaven, is not self-rejection or remorse, but the healing that comes from telling ourselves the truth about our real intentions, and finally, self-acceptance. This does not mean that we are now proud of who we were or what we did, but it does mean that we have taken what we did back into ourselves, acknowledged it as part of ourselves. We have found its original motive, realized how it became disfigured, perhaps beyond recognition, made real apologies, done our best to repair the injury, but we no longer try to reject who we have been and therefore who we are, for even that is an expression of the Holy One of Being.

We do not simply repudiate the evil we have done and sincerely mean never to do again; that is easy (we do it all the time). We receive whatever evils we have intended and done back into ourselves as our own deliberate creations. We cherish them as long-banished children finally taken home again. And thereby transform them and ourselves. When we say the *vidui,* the confession, we don't hit ourselves; we hold ourselves.

Lawrence Kushner[16]

On Simchat Torah we finish reading the Torah and begin again. The same is true with the Twelve Steps. It has been said that one can only work Step One all the way through. One works the other steps partially, a little each time, and must work them again and again.

Like Torah, the Twelve Steps represent an ongoing way of life, not a one-time experience.

Like Torah, the Twelve Steps experience is never complete.

As we work through and try to live by the Twelve Steps, as we study and are guided by the teachings of Torah, we grow spiritually. Each time we return to a particular Torah portion or to a different step, we see it from a different vantage point, peering further and deeper into Torah and ourselves.

Each week we concentrate on one Torah portion, but consider the entire Torah. Likewise, we work on all Twelve Steps all the time, although at any given time, we concentrate on only one.

A hint: if you have trouble with a particular step, don't skip it or beat your head against it. Go back and work through the earlier steps until you feel comfortable tackling the one that is causing you problems. And then begin again.

A PRAYER

In Judaism, we celebrate new beginnings with this prayer of thanks: *Baruch ata Adonai Elohenu Melech Ha-olam shehechayanu, vekeyimanu, vehigiyanu laazman hazeh.* Praised are You, Adonai our God, Sovereign of the Universe, who has sustained us and brought us forward so that we might reach this day. Amen.

CONTEMPORARY VOICES FOR RECOVERY

An all-encompassing conversation has been taking place since our people stood at Sinai. As we recognize that our lives are Torah, we see that we have been invited to join in this conversation not only to listen in respectful or awed silence, but to add our voice to the many that take part. The truth of our lives *enfleshes* the Torah and makes it relevant to the world of the historical period. The Torah stories didn't all happen once, a long, long time ago: they continue to happen, so now it is our turn to respond to the challenges they offer.

Carol Ochs[17]

REFLECTIONS

Moving from Here to Recovering: An Afterword

On a Sunday morning in October, Jews are weeping in the social hall of a fading resort in the Catskill Mountains. For the more than two hundred recovering alcoholics, addicts, and their loved ones in attendance, the tears of shame and remorse have vanished. On this final day of the autumn JACS Retreat, they are shedding tears of gratitude. Many have begun to relate to their Jewish identity and are letting go of feelings of alienation and ostracism from the community. There is the growing sense that the lifeline many discovered in a church basement is a fundamental part of their Jewish heritage, a discovery of wholeness and connection with a tradition that, for some, had lost its meaning and, for others, had little meaning at all.

Rabbi Olitzky and Dr. Copans have made a significant contribution to articulating the bond of Judaism and recovery. They put to rest once and for all the misconception of many that the Twelve Step recovery process is not compatible with Jewish tradition and belief. Most importantly, they made a substantial dent in the wall of denial that has plagued the Jewish community concerning the problem of substance abuse. This is a life-saving contribution, and many will be forever in their debt.

Their work underscores the advocacy role of JACS (Jewish Alcoholics, Chemically Dependent Persons, and Significant Others)—promoting the idea that the disease of addiction can happen to Jews, and that the age-old myth of Jewish immunity has hindered social service agencies, lay leadership, and the rabbinate from addressing the problem in an emphatic way. Under the prescient auspices of the UJA-Federation of Greater New York and United Way of New York, JACS has been endeavoring to dispel the myths, to dissolve the indifference and neglect by training, sensitizing, and speaking out within the Jewish community. Additionally, by providing programs for Jews recovering from alcoholism and chemical dependency, JACS has offered an opportunity for spiritual renewal and healing, an endeavor that has served as a model for an ever-growing number of grassroots organizations across the country.

Since the first Retreat in 1979, JACS has striven to provide an environment where Jewish self-discovery is accessible for all. The Retreat program, developed by the JACS membership, has no religious agenda, nor is one particular perspective represented as more praiseworthy than the next. Here the unaffiliated and the ultraorthodox come together as travelers on a similar journey. Though they may have embarked from different starting points, they share the same destination of Jewish spiritual fulfillment. This is Judaism at its most vital and expansive, an attitude shared at the gut level by all the participants, ripened by their experiences in the Twelve Step recovery fellowships of Alcoholics Anonymous, Narcotics Anonymous, Adult Children of Alcoholics, Al-Anon, and many others.

One cannot overemphasize the efficacy of the Twelve Step recovery movement. It is the focal point from which any serious discussion about long-term, successful abstinence from alcohol or drugs must derive. For family members, the Al-Anon and Nar-Anon programs offer the most enduring means for developing healthy skills for coping with both active and recovering substance abusers. Indeed, the success of the Anonymous programs has been so substantial, there are no reputable rehabilitation facilities that do not make attendance a mandatory component of the treatment process.

Nevertheless, it needs to be mentioned that confusion and misconceptions still abound. The success of Alcoholics Anonymous has spawned more than two hundred recovery programs, addressing a wide array of personal problems and concerns. The growing number of these opportunities has led in recent years to much media attention and intellectual scrutiny. Many of the resulting generalizations not only betray a lack of personal experience but a profound misunderstanding of the differences between self-help and self-pity, surrender and disempowerment, spirituality and religion, community and cult, or healing environment and therapeutic milieu. In truth, for the millions whose lives have been saved by Alcoholics Anonymous, it is much like grumbling about a speeding ambulance because it disrupts traffic.

These issues need to be addressed because this misinformation does a tremendous disservice to those in need of help. Addiction is a disease of denial, and the addict is usually the last to acknowledge his or her dependence. At the same time, rationalizations proliferate about seeking assistance. For most, the prospect of attending an AA meeting is tantamount to a deathbed confession, the last stop on a road of broken promises and diminishing self-respect. The confusion about religion and spiritual recovery is a particularly difficult roadblock, and, for Jews in need, a long history of community ignorance and indifference about the self-help program has made it especially troublesome.

Simply put, AA works. It works for everyone, regardless of background, who is willing to be completely honest about their drinking problem. The cornerstone of Alcoholics Anonymous, to use the primary example, is the fundamental philosophy of one drunk helping another, of a community of alcoholics who, as a result of their common problem, are able to share their experience, strength, and hope in the mutual desire to stay away from drinking one day at a time. This connection, this reaching out, is available twenty-four hours a day. The typical AA meeting emphasizes this openness. Occasionally there are tears. Sometimes anger. Yet it is a safe environment. Everyone understands. Here the only requirement for membership is a desire to stop drinking. Some meetings are held in church basements. Yet everyone, regardless of denomination, is welcome. Religious, cultural, or economic differences are simply not on the agenda. Most groups conclude the meeting with a prayer. But the intent is a communal expression of gratitude, not dogma, nor is a belief in God, or any other philosophy, a requirement for full participation. Some members augment their recovery with therapy. Others do not. But most are paying very close attention to how they can make their lives whole once again. At the center of this self-scrutiny are the Twelve Steps of recovery, and they, too, are not an obligatory part of the program. They are suggested as an opportunity for self-awareness and peace of mind. They are experiential and, over time, can become a natural expression of one's daily life. Most importantly, they are a foundation for continued growth. As Bill W., cofounder of Alcoholics Anonymous, once noted, "AA is a spiritual kindergarten." Whether one's personal development takes the form of religious renewal or psychological and spiritual insight, the intent is for ongoing and lifelong self-expansion.

The Twelve Steps emphasize spiritual and personal awareness, taking stock, reaching out to others in need. These are basic Jewish values, and they need to be exercised much more forcefully by the Jewish community in dealing with the problem of alcoholism and chemical dependency. Addiction is a disease, not a *shonda* (disgrace), and our priorities should demand action, not statistics, emphasis on remedies rather than bemoaning reasons why. Rabbi Olitzky and Dr. Copans have offered a thought-provoking guide for the growing number of people who are seeking to enhance the recovery process from the perspective of Jewish tradition and belief. At JACS we will continue to strive to see that more Jews be given that opportunity, that those who still suffer from addiction will find the resources they need within a community kindled by an age-old legacy of healing, compassion, and care.

Jeff Neipris, executive director;
David Buchholz, president
The JACS Foundation, Inc.

A Final Prayer

May you live to see your world fulfilled
May your destiny be for worlds still to
come
May you trust in generations past and yet
to be

May your eyes shine with the light of holy
words
And your face reflect the brightness of the
heavens
May your lips ever speak wisdom
Your fulfillment be in justice
Even as you ever yearn to listen to the
words of
The Holy Ancient One of old

May your heart be filled with intuition
And your words be filled with insight
May songs of praise be upon your tongue
Your vision straight before you
Even as you ever yearn to listen to the
words of
The Holy Ancient One of old

Babylonian Talmud, Berachot 17a,
translated by Lawrence Kushner

For Further Help

(and to find a local group in your community)

Al-Anon Family Group Headquarters, Inc.
1600 Corporate Landing Parkway
Virginia Beach, VA 23454-5617
757/563-1600
www.al-anon.alateen.org

Alateen
1600 Corporate Landing Parkway
Virginia Beach, VA 23454-5617
757/563-1600
www.al-anon.alateen.org

Alcoholics Anonymous World Services, Inc. (AA)
Mailing Address:
Box 459
New York, NY 10163
Location:
11th Floor
475 Riverside Drive at West 120th St.
New York, NY 10115
212/870-3400
www.aa.org

Beit T'Shuvah
8831 Venice Boulevard
Los Angeles, CA 90034
310/204-5200
www.beittshuvahla.org

Chabad Centers
Chabad Residential Treatment Center
5675 West Olympic Boulevard
Los Angeles, CA 90036
323/965-1365
www.chabad.org

Chabad Project Pride—Centre Lifeline
4985 Queen Mary Road
Montreal, Quebec H4W 1X4
Canada
514/485-5121
www.projectpride.org

CHAI-JACS
Jews in Recovery from Alcoholism and Drug
 Abuse
3701 W. Devon Ave.
Chicago, IL 60645
773/539-7779 or
847/679-1042

Cocaine Anonymous World Services (CA)

Mailing Address:
P.O. Box 492000
Los Angeles, CA 90049-8000
Location:
3740 Overland Avenue, Suite C
Los Angeles, CA 90034
310/559-5833
www.ca.org

Families Anonymous
P.O. Box 3475
Culver City, CA 90231-3475
800/736-9805
www.familiesanonymous.org

Friendship Recovery Homes
Daniel B. Sobel Friendship House
Meer Family Friendship Center
6892 West Maple Road
West Bloomfield, MI 48322
248/788-8888
www.friendshiprecoveryhomes.org

Gamblers Anonymous
International Service Office
P.O. Box 17173
Los Angeles, CA 90017
213/386-8789
www.gamblersanonymous.org

Hamayan Jewish Recovery Home
17950 Military Trail
Boca Raton, FL 33496
561/450-5503
www.chabad.org

JACS Foundation, Inc.
(Jewish Alcoholics, Chemically Dependent
 Persons, and Significant Others)
120 West 57th Street
New York, NY 10019
212/397-4197
www.jacsweb.org

Jewish Recovery Communities
www.chabad.org/library/article_cdo/aid/714476/
 jewish/Jewish-Recovery-Communities.htm

Jewish Recovery Houses
3723 Old Court Road, Suite 206
Pikesville, MD 21208
410/585-1223
www.jewishrecoveryhouses.org

Narcotics Anonymous (NA)
World Services Office
P.O. Box 9999
Van Nuys, CA 91409
818/773-9999

www.na.org

National Council on Alcoholism and Drug Dependence (NCADD)
244 East 58th Street, Fourth Floor
New York, NY 10022
212/269-7797 or
800/NCA-CALL
www.ncadd.org

National Self-Help Clearinghouse
365 Fifth Avenue, Suite 3300
New York, NY 10016
212/817-1822

Nicotine Anonymous
World Services Office
419 Main Street, PMB #370
Huntington Beach, CA 92648
415/750-0328 or
877/TRY-NICA
www.nicotine-anonymous.org

Overeaters Anonymous
Mailing Address:
P.O. Box 44020
Rio Rancho, NM 87174-4020
Location:
6075 Zenith Court NE

Rio Rancho, NM 87144-6424
505/891-2664;
www.oa.org

Pills Anonymous
Old Chelsea Station
P.O. Box 1972
New York, NY 10113
212/874-0700
www.pillsanonymous.info

Rodfei Shalom Fellowship
Florida Office:
8358 West Oakland Park Blvd.
Sunrise, FL 33351
954/485-0188
New York Office:
147-22 68th Avenue
Flushing, NY 11367
917/776-7574
www.rodfeishalom.org

Sexaholics Anonymous
P.O. Box 3565
Brentwood, TN 37024
615/370-6062 or
866/424-8777
www.sa.org

Sex and Love Addicts Anonymous
1550 NE Loop 410, Suite 118
San Antonio, TX 78209
210/828-7900
www.slaafws.org

Survivors of Incest Anonymous
World Services Office
P.O. Box 190
Benson, MD 21018
410/893-3322
www.siawso.org

Yatzkan Center Residential Program
Chemical Dependency for Youth
15-19 Duryea Place
Brooklyn, NY 11226
718/282-2504
www.yatzkan.org

Notes

[1]   Abraham J. Twerski, "AA Is Not For Me," in *How to Respond* (Aliquippa, Penn.: Gateway Publications, 1986).

[2]   We have quoted here the original AA language, which uses the masculine pronoun in referring to God. Like many other Twelve Step programs, we try to avoid using gendered pronouns that refer to God, who we believe incorporates—and transcends—the characteristics attributed to both sexes.

[3]   God is known by many names in Jewish tradition. Since we really do not know how to pronounce God's essential name, we generally use Adonai (literally "Lord") to refer to God.

[4]   Lionel Blue and Jonathan Magonet, *How to Get Up When Life Gets You Down: A Companion and Guide* (London: Fount, 1992), 143.

[5]   The addict spends so much money on drugs pumped into his/her arm that it is as if the arm is made out of gold.

[6]   Harold M. Schulweis, *For Those Who Can't Believe: Overcoming the Obstacles to Faith* (New York: HarperCollins, 1995), 43.

[7]   David Wolpe, *Making Loss Matter: Creating Meaning in Difficult Times* (New York: Riverhead, 1999), 123–124.

[8]   Karyn D. Kedar, *The Bridge to Forgiveness: Stories and Prayers for Finding God and Restoring Wholeness* (Woodstock, Vt.: Jewish Lights, 2007), 23.

[9]   Daniel Gordis, *God Was Not in the Fire: The Search for a Spiritual Judaism* (New York: Simon & Schuster, 1997), 223.

[10]   Ira F. Stone, "God," in *The Jewish Lights Spirituality Handbook: A Guide to Understanding, Exploring, & Living a Spiritual Life,* ed. Stuart M. Matlins (Woodstock, Vt.: Jewish Lights, 2001), 33.

[11]   Merle Feld, *A Spiritual Life: A Jewish Feminist Journey* (Albany, N.Y.: State University of New York Press, 2000), 238.

[12]   Shoni Labowitz, *Miraculous Living: A Guided Journey in Kabbalah through the Ten Gates of the Tree of Life* (New York: Simon and Schuster, 1996), 118.

[13]   Rami Shapiro, *The Way of Solomon: Finding Joy and Contentment in the Wisdom of Ecclesiastes* (San Francisco: HarperSanFrancisco, 2000), 132–133.

[14]   Harold Kushner, *How Good Do We Have to Be? A New Understanding of Guilt and*

Forgiveness (New York: Little, Brown, 1996), 174.

[15] Norman Cohen, *Self, Struggle and Change: Family Conflict Stories in Genesis and Their Healing Insights for Our Lives.* (Woodstock, Vt.: Jewish Lights, 1995), 81.

[16] Lawrence Kushner, *God Was in This Place and I, i Did Not Know: Finding Self, Spirituality and Ultimate Meaning* (Woodstock, Vt.: Jewish Lights, 1991), 79–80.

[17] Carol Ochs, *Our Lives as Torah: Finding God in Our Own Stories* (San Francisco: Jossey-Bass, 2001), 2.

Glossary of Important Words and Concepts

Adonai: God is known by various names in Jewish tradition. Adonai (literally "Lord") is used to refer to God since we do not know how to (and dare not) pronounce God's essential name

cheshbon hanefesh: a probing inventory of the soul, taken by individuals especially prior to the High Holidays

Covenant: the agreement established some 3,200 years ago between God and the people of Israel at Sinai

Elul: the month prior to the High Holidays (usually late August to early September), which focuses on introspection, repentance, and renewal

mitzvah/mitzvot: divine commandments given by God to the Jewish people

shalom: wholeness and completeness, epitomized by peace

teshuvah: literally a turning toward God and a righteous, religious way of life; in a broader sense, this represents returning and moving toward recovering

tzedakah: charitable giving usually of substance but also of self

Yom Kippur: Day of Atonement; according to many the holiest day of the year, this Holy Day is also called the Sabbath of Sabbaths.

More than any other time on the Jewish calendar, it epitomizes the focus on introspection, repentance, and renewal

Selected Readings

Elkins, Dov Peretz, ed. *Rosh Hashanah Readings: Inspiration, Information and Contemplation.* Woodstock, Vt.: Jewish Lights, 2006.

_____. *Yom Kippur Readings: Inspiration, Information and Contemplation.* Woodstock, Vt.: Jewish Lights, 2005.

Gefen, Nan Fink. *Jewish Meditation: How to Begin Your Practice.* LifeLights series. Woodstock, Vt.: Jewish Lights, 2002.

Goldstein, Elyse, ed. *The Women's Haftarah Commentary: New Insights from Women Rabbis on the Fifty-four Weekly Haftarah Portions, the Five Megillot and Special Shabbatot.* Woodstock, Vt.: Jewish Lights, 2004.

_____. *The Women's Torah Commentary: New Insights from Women Rabbis on the Fifty-four Weekly Torah Portions.* Woodstock, Vt.: Jewish Lights, 2000.

Hendler, Lee Meyerhoff. *The Year Mom Got Religion: One Woman's Midlife Journey into Judaism.* Woodstock, Vt.: Jewish Lights, 1999.

Heschel, Abraham Joshua. *The Sabbath.* New York: Farrar, Straus and Giroux, 2005.

Jewish Board of Family and Children's Services. *Jewish Sisters in Sobriety: Jewish Women's Untold Stories of Alcoholism, Drug Addiction, Co-Dependence and Recovery.* New York: Jewish Board of Family and Children's Services, 2007.

Jewish Publication Society of America. *The Book of Psalms: A New Translation According to the Traditional Hebrew Text.* Philadelphia: Jewish Publication Society of America, 1997.

Kedar, Karyn D. *The Bridge to Forgiveness: Stories and Prayers for Finding God and Restoring Wholeness.* Woodstock, Vt.: Jewish Lights, 2007.

_____. *God Whispers: Stories of the Soul, Lessons of the Heart.* Woodstock, Vt.: Jewish Lights, 1999.

Kula, Irwin, and Vanessa L. Ochs, eds. *The Book of Jewish Sacred Practices: CLAL's Guide to Everyday and Holiday Rituals and Blessings.* Woodstock, Vt.: Jewish Lights, 2001.

Kushner, Lawrence. *God Was in This Place and I, i Did Not Know: Finding Self, Spirituality and Ultimate Meaning.* Woodstock, Vt.: Jewish Lights, 1991.

_____. *Honey from the Rock: An Introduction to Jewish Mysticism.* Woodstock, Vt.: Jewish Lights, 2000.

Matlins, Stuart M., ed. *The Jewish Lights Spirituality Handbook: A Guide to Understanding, Exploring and Living a Spiritual Life.* Woodstock, Vt.: Jewish Lights, 2001.

Meszler, Joseph B. *A Man's Responsibility: A Jewish Guide to Being a Son, a Partner in Marriage, a Father and a Community Leader.* Woodstock, Vt.: Jewish Lights, 2008.

Mykoff, Moshe, and the Breslov Research Institute. *The Empty Chair: Finding Hope and Joy—Timeless Wisdom from a Hasidic Master,*

Rebbe Nachman of Breslov. Woodstock, Vt.: Jewish Lights, 1996.

_____, and S.C. Mizrahi. *The Gentle Weapon: Prayers for Everyday and Not-So-Everyday Moments—Timeless Wisdom from the Teachings of the Hasidic Master, Rebbe Nachman of Breslov.* Woodstock, Vt.: Jewish Lights, 1999.

Olitzky, Kerry M. *Life's Daily Blessings: Inspiring Reflections on Gratitude and Joy for Every Day, Based on Jewish Wisdom.* Woodstock, Vt.: Jewish Lights, 2009.

_____. *One Hundred Blessings Every Day: Daily Twelve Step Recovery Affirmations, Exercises for Personal Growth and Renewal Reflecting Seasons of the Jewish Year.* Woodstock, Vt.: Jewish Lights, 1993.

_____. *Recovery from Codependence: A Jewish Twelve Steps Guide to Healing Your Soul.* Woodstock, Vt.: Jewish Lights, 1993.

_____, and Lori Forman. *Restful Reflections: Nighttime Inspiration to Calm the Soul, Based on Jewish Wisdom.* Woodstock, Vt.: Jewish Lights, 2001.

144

_____, and Lori Forman. *Sacred Intentions: Daily Inspiration to Strengthen the Spirit, Based on Jewish Wisdom.* Woodstock, Vt.: Jewish Lights, 1999.

_____, and Daniel Judson, eds. *The Rituals and Practices of a Jewish Life: A Handbook for Personal Spiritual Renewal.* Woodstock, Vt.: Jewish Lights, 2002.

_____, and Aaron Z. *Renewed Each Day: Daily Twelve Step Recovery Meditations Based on the Bible (Vol.1—Genesis and Exodus, Vol.2—Leviticus, Numbers and Deuteronomy).* Woodstock, Vt.: Jewish Lights, 1992.

Roth, Jeff. *Jewish Meditation Practices for Everyday Life: Awakening Your Heart, Connecting with God.* Woodstock, Vt.: Jewish Lights, 2009.

Salkin, Jeffrey K., ed. *The Modern Men's Torah Commentary: New Insights from Jewish Men on the Fifty-four Weekly Torah Portions.* Woodstock, Vt.: Jewish Lights, 2009.

Shapiro, Rami. *Recovery—The Sacred Art: The Twelve Steps as Spiritual Practice.* Woodstock, Vt.: SkyLight Paths, 2009.

Spitz, Elie Kaplan, and Erica Shapiro Taylor. *Healing from Despair: Choosing Wholeness in a Broken World.* Woodstock, Vt.: Jewish Lights, 2008.

Steinberg, Milton. *As a Driven Leaf.* West Orange, N.J.: Behrman House, 1996.

Strassfeld, Michael. *A Book of Life: Embracing Judaism as a Spiritual Practice.* Woodstock, Vt.: Jewish Lights, 2002.

Twerski, Abraham J. *A Formula for Proper Living: Practical Lessons from Life and Torah.* Woodstock, Vt.: Jewish Lights, 2009.

_____. *Happiness and the Human Spirit: The Spirituality of Becoming the Best You Can Be.* Woodstock, Vt.: Jewish Lights, 2007.

_____. *Living Each Day.* Brooklyn, N.Y.: Mesorah, 1988.

146

_____. *Recognizing a Loved One's Addiction, and Providing Help.* LifeLights series. Woodstock, Vt.: Jewish Lights, 2003.

_____. *Self-Discovery in Recovery.* San Francisco: HarperCollins, 1989.

_____. *Waking Up Just in Time.* New York: St. Martin's Griffin, 1995.

_____. *When Do the Good Things Start?* New York: St. Martin's Griffin, 1995.

About the Illustrations

Artist Maty Grünberg's Illustrations of the gates of the Old City of Jerusalem open each chapter of the Twelve Steps, welcoming the reader into another stage of a Jewish Twelve Steps experience. These were selected to emphasize the relationship between the heavenly and the earthly in all our lives through the prism of Jerusalem.

One enters a different plane of reality both physically and spiritually when entering the gates of the Old City. Our lives were changed by Jerusalem. Recognizing that at the center of the Jewish spiritual world is Jerusalem, we invited Maty Grünberg to draw the gates of his beloved city so that you might enter it also, one gate at a time.

148

Theology/Philosophy

A Touch of the Sacred: A Theologian's Informal Guide to Jewish Belief
By Dr. Eugene B. Borowitz and Frances W. Schwartz
Explores the musings from the leading theologian of liberal Judaism.

Talking about God: Exploring the Meaning of Religious Life with Kierkegaard, Buber, Tillich and Heschel *By Daniel F. Polish, PhD*
Examines the meaning of the human religious experience with the greatest theologians of modern times.
(A book from SkyLight Paths, Jewish Lights' sister imprint)

Jews & Judaism in the 21st Century: Human Responsibility, the Presence of God, and the Future of the Covenant *Edited by Rabbi Edward Feinstein; Foreword by Paula E. Hyman* Five celebrated leaders in Judaism examine contemporary Jewish life.

Christians and Jews in Dialogue: Learning in the Presence of the Other
By Mary C. Boys and Sara S. Lee; Foreword by Dr. Dorothy Bass

(A book from SkyLight Paths, Jewish Lights' sister imprint)
The Death of Death: Resurrection and Immortality in Jewish Thought
By Neil Gillman

Ethics of the Sages: *Pirke Avot*—Annotated & Explained
Translation & Annotation by Rabbi Rami Shapiro
(A book from SkyLight Paths, Jewish Lights' sister imprint)

Hasidic Tales: Annotated & Explained *By Rabbi Rami Shapiro; Foreword by Andrew Harvey*
(A book from SkyLight Paths, Jewish Lights' sister imprint)

A Heart of Many Rooms: Celebrating the Many Voices within Judaism
By David Hartman

The Hebrew Prophets: Selections Annotated & Explained
Translation & Annotation by Rabbi Rami Shapiro; Foreword by Zalman M. Schachter-Shalomi
(A book from SkyLight Paths, Jewish Lights' sister imprint)

A Jewish Understanding of the New Testament
By Rabbi Samuel Sandmel; Preface by Rabbi David Sandmel
(A book from SkyLight Paths, Jewish Lights' sister imprint)

Keeping Faith with the Psalms: Deepen Your Relationship with God Using the Book of Psalms *By Daniel F. Polish*

A Living Covenant: The Innovative Spirit in Traditional Judaism
By David Hartman

Love and Terror in the God Encounter: The Theological Legacy of Rabbi Joseph B. Soloveitchik *By David Hartman*

The Personhood of God: Biblical Theology, Human Faith and the Divine Image
By Dr. Yochanan Muffs; Foreword by Dr. David Hartman

Traces of God: Seeing God in Torah, History and Everyday Life *By Neil Gillman*

We Jews and Jesus: Exploring Theological Differences for Mutual Understanding
By Rabbi Samuel Sandmel; Preface by Rabbi David Sandmel
(A book from SkyLight Paths, Jewish Lights' sister imprint)

Your Word Is Fire: The Hasidic Masters on Contemplative Prayer
Edited and translated by Arthur Green and Barry W. Holtz

I Am Jewish
Personal Reflections Inspired by the Last Words of Daniel Pearl
Almost 150 Jews—both famous and not—from all walks of life, from all around the world, write about many aspects of their Judaism.
Edited by Judea and Ruth Pearl
Download a free copy of the *I Am Jewish Teacher's Guide* at our website:
www.jewishlights.com

Congregation Resources

Building a Successful Volunteer Culture
Finding Meaning in Service in the Jewish Community
By Rabbi Charles Simon; Foreword by Shelley Lindauer; Preface by Dr. Ron Wolfson
Shows you how to develop and maintain the volunteers who are essential to the vitality of your organization and community.

The Case for Jewish Peoplehood: Can We Be One?
By Dr. Erica Brown and Dr. Misha Galperin; Foreword by Rabbi Joseph Telushkin
Explores the purpose, possibilities, and limitations of peoplehood as a unifying concept of community for a people struggling profoundly with Jewish identity.

Finding a Spiritual Home: How a New Generation of Jews Can Transform the American Synagogue *By Rabbi Sidney Schwarz*

Inspired Jewish Leadership: Practical Approaches to Building Strong Communities
By Dr. Erica Brown

Jewish Pastoral Care, 2nd Edition: A Practical Handbook from Traditional & Contemporary Sources *Edited by Rabbi Dayle A. Friedman, MSW, MAJCS, BCC*

Jewish Spiritual Direction: An Innovative Guide from Traditional and Contemporary Sources *Edited by Rabbi Howard A. Addison and Barbara Eve Breitman*

Rethinking Synagogues: A New Vocabulary for Congregational Life
By Rabbi Lawrence A. Hoffman

Spiritual Community: The Power to Restore Hope, Commitment and Joy
By Rabbi David A. Teutsch, PhD

The Spirituality of Welcoming: How to Transform Your Congregation into a Sacred Community *By Dr. Ron Wolfson*

Children's Books

What You Will See Inside a Synagogue
By Rabbi Lawrence A. Hoffman and Dr. Ron Wolfson; Full-color photos by Bill Aron
A colorful, fun-to-read introduction that explains the ways and whys of Jewish worship and religious life.
For ages 6 & up (A book from SkyLight Paths, Jewish Lights' sister imprint)

Because Nothing Looks Like God
By Lawrence and Karen Kushner Introduces children to the possibilities of spiritual life.
For ages 4 & up

Board Book Companions to Because Nothing Looks Like God
SkyLight Paths Board Books For ages 0–4

What Does God Look Like?

How Does God Make Things Happen?

Where Is God?

The Book of Miracles: A Young Person's Guide to Jewish Spiritual Awareness
By Lawrence Kushner. All-new illustrations by the author
For ages 9 and up

In God's Hands
By Lawrence Kushner and Gary Schmidt

In Our Image: God's First Creatures *By Nancy Sohn Swartz*
For ages 4 & up

Also Available as a Board Book: **How Did the Animals Help God?**
For ages 0–4

(A book from SkyLight Paths, Jewish Lights' sister imprint)

The Kids' Fun Book of Jewish Time
By Emily Sper

What Makes Someone a Jew? *By Lauren Seidman*
Reflects the changing face of American Judaism.

For ages 3–6

152

Current Events/History

A Dream of Zion: American Jews Reflect on Why Israel Matters to Them
Edited by Rabbi Jeffrey K. Salkin Explores what Jewish people in America have to say about Israel.
  Also Available: **A Dream of Zion Teacher's Guide**

The Ethiopian Jews of Israel: Personal Stories of Life in the Promised Land *By Len Lyons, PhD; Foreword by Alan Dershowitz; Photographs by Ilan Ossendryver*
Recounts, through photographs and words, stories of Ethiopian Jews.

Foundations of Sephardic Spirituality: The Inner Life of Jews of the Ottoman Empire
  By Rabbi Marc D. Angel, PhD

Hannah Senesh: Her Life and Diary, the First Complete Edition
  By Hannah Senesh; Foreword by Marge Piercy; Preface by Eitan Senesh; Afterword by Roberta Grossman

The Jewish Connection to Israel, the Promised Land: A Brief Introduction for Christians *By Rabbi Eugene Korn, PhD*

Judaism and Justice: The Jewish Passion to Repair the World
  By Rabbi Sidney Schwarz

The Story of the Jews: A 4,000-Year Adventure—A Graphic History Book
  Written & illustrated by Stan Mack

Ecology/Environment

A Wild Faith: Jewish Ways into Wilderness, Wilderness Ways into Judaism
By Rabbi Mike Comins; Foreword by Nigel Savage
Offers ways to enliven and deepen your spiritual life through wilderness experience.

Ecology & the Jewish Spirit: Where Nature & the Sacred Meet
  Edited by Ellen Bernstein

Torah of the Earth: Exploring 4,000 Years of Ecology in Jewish Thought
  Vol. 1: Biblical Israel: One Land, One People; Rabbinic Judaism: One People, Many Lands
  Vol. 2: Zionism: One Land, Two Peoples; Eco-Judaism: One Earth, Many Peoples
  Edited by Arthur Waskow Vol. 1:
  Vol. 2:

The Way Into Judaism and the Environment *By Jeremy Benstein, PhD*

Grief/Healing

Healing and the Jewish Imagination: Spiritual and Practical Perspectives on Judaism and Health *Edited by Rabbi William Cutter, PhD*
Explores Judaism for comfort in times of illness and perspectives on suffering.

Grief in Our Seasons: A Mourner's Kaddish Companion *By Rabbi Kerry M. Olitzky*

Healing of Soul, Healing of Body: Spiritual Leaders Unfold the Strength & Solace in Psalms *Edited by Rabbi Simkha Y. Weintraub, CSW*

Mourning & Mitzvah, 2nd Edition: A Guided Journal for Walking the Mourner's Path through Grief to Healing *By Anne Brener, LCSW*

Tears of Sorrow, Seeds of Hope, 2nd Edition: A Jewish Spiritual Companion for Infertility and Pregnancy Loss *By Rabbi Nina Beth Cardin*

A Time to Mourn, a Time to Comfort, 2nd Edition: A Guide to Jewish Bereavement *By Dr. Ron Wolfson*

When a Grandparent Dies: A Kid's Own Remembering Workbook for Dealing with Shiva and the Year Beyond *By Nechama Liss-Levinson, PhD*
                                         For ages 7–13

Life Cycle
Marriage / Parenting / Family / Aging

The New Jewish Baby Album: Creating and Celebrating the Beginning of a Spiritual Life—A Jewish Lights Companion
By the Editors at Jewish Lights. Foreword by Anita Diamant. Preface by Rabbi Sandy Eisenberg Sasso.
A spiritual keepsake that will be treasured for generations. More than just a memory book, *shows you how—and why it's important*—to create a Jewish home and a Jewish life.

The Jewish Pregnancy Book: A Resource for the Soul, Body & Mind during Pregnancy, Birth & the First Three Months
By Sandy Falk, MD, and Rabbi Daniel Judson, with Steven A. Rapp
Includes medical information, prayers and rituals for each stage of pregnancy, from a liberal Jewish perspective.

Celebrating Your New Jewish Daughter: Creating Jewish Ways to Welcome Baby Girls into the Covenant—New and Traditional Ceremonies *By Debra Nussbaum Cohen; Foreword by Rabbi Sandy Eisenberg Sasso*

The New Jewish Baby Book, 2nd Edition: Names, Ceremonies & Customs—A Guide for Today's Families *By Anita Diamant*

Parenting as a Spiritual Journey: Deepening Ordinary and Extraordinary Events into Sacred Occasions *By Rabbi Nancy Fuchs-Kreimer*

Parenting Jewish Teens: A Guide for the Perplexed
By Joanne Doades
Explores the questions and issues that shape the world in which today's Jewish teenagers live.

Judaism for Two: A Spiritual Guide for Strengthening and Celebrating Your Loving Relationship
By Rabbi Nancy Fuchs-Kreimer and Rabbi Nancy H. Wiener; Foreword by Rabbi Elliot N. Dorff
Addresses the ways Jewish teachings can enhance and strengthen committed relationships.

The Creative Jewish Wedding Book, 2nd Edition: A Hands-On Guide to New & Old Traditions, Ceremonies & Celebrations *By Gabrielle Kaplan-Mayer*

Divorce Is a Mitzvah: A Practical Guide to Finding Wholeness and Holiness When Your Marriage Dies *By Rabbi Perry Netter; Afterword by Rabbi Laura Geller.*

Embracing the Covenant: Converts to Judaism Talk About Why & How
By Rabbi Allan Berkowitz and Patti Moskovitz

The Guide to Jewish Interfaith Family Life: An InterfaithFamily.com Handbook *Edited by Ronnie Friedland and Edmund Case*

A Heart of Wisdom: Making the Jewish Journey from Midlife through the Elder Years *Edited by Susan Berrin; Foreword by Harold Kushner*

Introducing My Faith and My Community
The Jewish Outreach Institute Guide for the Christian in a Jewish Interfaith Relationship
By Rabbi Kerry M. Olitzky

Making a Successful Jewish Interfaith Marriage: The Jewish Outreach Institute Guide to Opportunities, Challenges and Resources *By Rabbi Kerry M. Olitzky with Joan Peterson Littman*

So That Your Values Live On: Ethical Wills and How to Prepare Them
Edited by Jack Riemer and Nathaniel Stampfer

Meditation

Jewish Meditation Practices for Everyday Life
Awakening Your Heart, Connecting with God
By Rabbi Jeff Roth
Offers a fresh take on meditation that draws on life experience and living life with greater clarity as opposed to the traditional method of rigorous study.

The Handbook of Jewish Meditation Practices
A Guide for Enriching the Sabbath and Other Days of Your Life
By Rabbi David A. Cooper Easy-to-learn meditation techniques.

Discovering Jewish Meditation: Instruction & Guidance for Learning an Ancient Spiritual Practice *By Nan Fink Gefen*

Meditation from the Heart of Judaism: Today's Teachers Share Their Practices, Techniques, and Faith *Edited by Avram Davis*

Ritual/Sacred Practice

The Jewish Dream Book: The Key to Opening the Inner Meaning of Your Dreams *By Vanessa L. Ochs with Elizabeth Ochs; Full-color illus. by Kristina Swarner*
Instructions for how modern people can perform ancient Jewish dream practices and dream interpretations drawn from the Jewish wisdom tradition.

God in Your Body: Kabbalah, Mindfulness and Embodied Spiritual Practice
By Jay Michaelson
The first comprehensive treatment of the body in Jewish spiritual practice and an essential guide to the sacred.

The Book of Jewish Sacred Practices: CLAL's Guide to Everyday & Holiday Rituals & Blessings *Edited by Rabbi Irwin Kula and Vanessa L. Ochs, PhD*

Jewish Ritual: A Brief Introduction for Christians
By Rabbi Kerry M. Olitzky and Rabbi Daniel Judson

The Rituals & Practices of a Jewish Life: A Handbook for Personal Spiritual Renewal *Edited by Rabbi Kerry M. Olitzky and Rabbi Daniel Judson*

The Sacred Art of Lovingkindness: Preparing to Practice
By Rabbi Rami Shapiro
(A book from SkyLight Paths, Jewish Lights' sister imprint)

Science Fiction/Mystery & Detective Fiction

Criminal Kabbalah: An Intriguing Anthology of Jewish Mystery & Detective Fiction *Edited by Lawrence W. Raphael; Foreword by Laurie R. King*
All-new stories from twelve of today's masters of mystery and detective fiction—sure to delight mystery buffs of all faith traditions.

Mystery Midrash: An Anthology of Jewish Mystery & Detective Fiction
Edited by Lawrence W. Raphael; Preface by Joel Siegel

Wandering Stars: An Anthology of Jewish Fantasy & Science Fiction
Edited by Jack Dann; Introduction by Isaac Asimov

More Wandering Stars: An Anthology of Outstanding Stories of Jewish Fantasy and Science Fiction *Edited by Jack Dann; Introduction by Isaac Asimov*

Spirituality/Lawrence Kushner

The Book of Letters: A Mystical Hebrew Alphabet
Popular HC Edition,
Collector's Limited Edition,

The Book of Miracles: A Young Person's Guide to Jewish Spiritual Awareness
For ages 9 and up
The Book of Words: Talking Spiritual Life, Living Spiritual Talk

Eyes Remade for Wonder: A Lawrence Kushner Reader *Introduction by Thomas Moore*

Filling Words with Light: Hasidic and Mystical Reflections on Jewish Prayer
By Lawrence Kushner and Nehemia Polen

God Was in This Place & I, i Did Not Know: Finding Self, Spirituality and
Ultimate Meaning
Honey from the Rock: An Introduction to Jewish Mysticism

Invisible Lines of Connection: Sacred Stories of the Ordinary

Jewish Spirituality—A Brief Introduction for Christians

The River of Light: Jewish Mystical Awareness

The Way Into Jewish Mystical Tradition

Spirituality/Prayer

My People's Passover Haggadah: Traditional Texts, Modern Commentaries
Edited by Rabbi Lawrence A. Hoffman, PhD, and David Arnow, PhD Diverse commentaries
on the traditional Passover Haggadah—in two volumes! Vol. 1:
Vol. 2:

Witnesses to the One: The Spiritual History of the *Sh'ma* *By Rabbi Joseph B. Meszler;*
Foreword by Rabbi Elyse Goldstein

My People's Prayer Book Series
Traditional Prayers, Modern Commentaries *Edited by Rabbi Lawrence A. Hoffman*
Provides diverse and exciting commentary to the traditional liturgy, helping modern
men and women find new wisdom in Jewish prayer, and bring liturgy into their lives.
Each book includes Hebrew text, modern translation, and commentaries from all
perspectives of the Jewish world.
Vol. 1—The *Sh'ma* and Its Blessings

Vol. 2—The *Amidah*

Vol. 3—*P'sukei D'zimrah* (Morning Psalms)

Vol. 4—*Seder K'riat Hatorah* (The Torah Service)

Vol. 5—*Birkhot Hashachar* (Morning Blessings)

Vol. 6—*Tachanun* and Concluding Prayers

Vol. 7—Shabbat at Home

Vol. 8—*Kabbalat Shabbat* (Welcoming Shabbat in the Synagogue)

Vol. 9—Welcoming the Night: *Minchah* and *Ma'ariv* (Afternoon and
Evening Prayer)
Vol. 10—Shabbat Morning: *Shacharit* and *Musaf* (Morning and
Additional Services)

Spirituality

Journeys to a Jewish Life: Inspiring Stories from the Spiritual Journeys of American Jews *By Paula Amann*
Examines the soul treks of Jews lost and found.

The Adventures of Rabbi Harvey: A Graphic Novel of Jewish Wisdom and Wit in the Wild West *By Steve Sheinkin*
Jewish and American folktales combine in this witty and original graphic novel collection. Creatively retold and set on the western frontier of the 1870s.

Rabbi Harvey Rides Again
A Graphic Novel of Jewish Folktales Let Loose in the Wild West *By Steve Sheinkin*

Ethics of the Sages: *Pirke Avot*—Annotated & Explained
Translation and Annotation by Rabbi Rami Shapiro
$16.99 *(A book from SkyLight Paths, Jewish Lights' sister imprint)*

A Book of Life: Embracing Judaism as a Spiritual Practice
By Michael Strassfeld

Meaning and Mitzvah: Daily Practices for Reclaiming Judaism through Prayer, God, Torah, Hebrew, Mitzvot and Peoplehood *By Rabbi Goldie Milgram*

The Soul of the Story: Meetings with Remarkable People
By Rabbi David Zeller

Aleph-Bet Yoga: Embodying the Hebrew Letters for Physical and Spiritual Well-Being
By Steven A. Rapp. Foreword by Tamar Frankiel, PhD and Judy Greenfeld. Preface by Hart Lazer.

Does the Soul Survive? A Jewish Journey to Belief in Afterlife, Past Lives & Living with Purpose *By Rabbi Elie Kaplan Spitz; Foreword by Brian L Weiss, MD*

First Steps to a New Jewish Spirit: Reb Zalman's Guide to Recapturing the Intimacy & Ecstasy in Your Relationship with God *By Rabbi Zalman M. Schachter-Shalomi with Donald Gropman*

God in Our Relationships: Spirituality between People from the Teachings of Martin Buber *By Rabbi Dennis S. Ross*

Judaism, Physics and God: Searching for Sacred Metaphors in a Post-Einstein World
By Rabbi David W. Nelson

The Jewish Lights Spirituality Handbook: A Guide to Understanding, Exploring & Living a Spiritual Life *Edited by Stuart M. Matlins*
What exactly is "Jewish" about spirituality? How do I make it a part of my life? Fifty of today's foremost spiritual leaders share their ideas and experience with us.

Bringing the Psalms to Life: How to Understand and Use the Book of Psalms
By Daniel F. Polish

God & the Big Bang: Discovering Harmony between Science & Spirituality
By Daniel C. Matt

Minding the Temple of the Soul: Balancing Body, Mind, and Spirit through Traditional Jewish Prayer, Movement, and Meditation *By Tamar Frankiel, PhD, and Judy Greenfeld*

One God Clapping: The Spiritual Path of a Zen Rabbi *By Alan Lew with Sherril Jaffe*

There Is No Messiah ... and You're It: The Stunning Transformation of Judaism's Most Provocative Idea *By Rabbi Robert N. Levine, DD*

These Are the Words: A Vocabulary of Jewish Spiritual Life
By Arthur Green

Inspiration

The Seven Questions You're Asked in Heaven: Reviewing and Renewing Your Life on Earth *By Dr. Ron Wolfson*
An intriguing and entertaining resource for living a life that matters.

Happiness and the Human Spirit: The Spirituality of Becoming the Best You Can Be *By Abraham J. Twerski, MD*
Shows you that true happiness is attainable once you stop looking outside yourself for the source.

Life's Daily Blessings: Inspiring Reflections on Gratitude and Joy for Every Day, Based on Jewish Wisdom *By Rabbi Kerry M. Olitzky*

The Bridge to Forgiveness: Stories and Prayers for Finding God and Restoring Wholeness *By Rabbi Karyn D. Kedar*
Examines how forgiveness can be the bridge that connects us to wholeness and peace.

God's To-Do List: 103 Ways to Be an Angel and Do God's Work on Earth *By Dr. Ron Wolfson*

Our Dance with God: Finding Prayer, Perspective and Meaning in the Stories of Our Lives *By Karyn D. Kedar*
Also Available: **The Dance of the Dolphin** (HC edition of Our Dance with God)

The Empty Chair: Finding Hope and Joy—Timeless Wisdom from a Hasidic Master, Rebbe Nachman of Breslov *Adapted by Moshe Mykoff and the Breslov Research Institute*

The Gentle Weapon: Prayers for Everyday and Not-So-Everyday Moments— Timeless Wisdom from the Teachings of the Hasidic Master, Rebbe Nachman of Breslov *Adapted by Moshe Mykoff and S. C. Mizrahi, together with the Breslov Research Institute*

God Whispers: Stories of the Soul, Lessons of the Heart *By Karyn D. Kedar*

Restful Reflections: Nighttime Inspiration to Calm the Soul, Based on Jewish Wisdom *By Rabbi Kerry M. Olitzky & Rabbi Lori Forman*

Sacred Intentions: Daily Inspiration to Strengthen the Spirit, Based on Jewish Wisdom *By Rabbi Kerry M. Olitzky and Rabbi Lori Forman*

Kabbalah/Mysticism

Seek My Face: A Jewish Mystical Theology *By Arthur Green*

Zohar: Annotated & Explained *Translation and annotation by Daniel C. Matt; Foreword by Andrew Harvey*
(A book from SkyLight Paths, Jewish Lights' sister imprint)

Ehyeh: A Kabbalah for Tomorrow *By Arthur Green*

The Flame of the Heart: Prayers of a Chasidic Mystic *By Reb Noson of Breslov. Translated by David Sears with the Breslov Research Institute*

The Gift of Kabbalah: Discovering the Secrets of Heaven, Renewing Your Life on Earth *By Tamar Frankiel, PhD*

Kabbalah: A Brief Introduction for Christians *By Tamar Frankiel, PhD*

The Lost Princess and Other Kabbalistic Tales of Rebbe Nachman of Breslov
The Seven Beggars and Other Kabbalistic Tales of Rebbe Nachman of Breslov
Translated by Rabbi Aryeh Kaplan; Preface by Rabbi Chaim Kramer
Lost Princess:
Seven Beggars:

See also *The Way Into Jewish Mystical Tradition* in Spirituality / Lawrence Kushner

Twelve Steps

100 Blessings Every Day: Daily Twelve Step Recovery Affirmations, Exercises for Personal Growth & Renewal Reflecting Seasons of the Jewish Year
By Rabbi Kerry M. Olitzky; Foreword by Rabbi Neil Gillman

Recovery—The Sacred Art: The Twelve Steps as Spiritual Practice
By Rami Shapiro
(A book from SkyLight Paths, Jewish Lights' sister imprint)

Recovery from Codependence: A Jewish Twelve Steps Guide to Healing Your Soul
By Rabbi Kerry M. Olitzky

Renewed Each Day: Daily Twelve Step Recovery Meditations
By Rabbi Kerry M. Olitzky & Aaron Z.
Vol. I—Genesis & Exodus
Introduction by Rabbi Michael A. Signer; Afterword by JACS Foundation

Vol. 2—Leviticus, Numbers & Deuteronomy
Introduction by Sharon M. Strassfeld; Afterword by Rabbi Harold M. Schulweis

Twelve Jewish Steps to Recovery, 2nd Edition: A Personal Guide to Turning from Alcoholism & Other Addictions—Drugs, Food, Gambling, Sex ...
By Rabbi Kerry M. Olitzky and Stuart A. Copans, MD; Preface by Abraham J. Twerski, MD

Spirituality / Crafts
(from SkyLight Paths, Jewish Lights sister imprint)

Beading—The Creative Spirit: Finding Your Sacred Center through the Art of Beadwork *by Rev. Wendy Ellsworth*
Invites you on a spiritual pilgrimage into the kaleidoscope world of glass and color.

Contemplative Crochet: A Hands-On Guide for Interlocking Faith and Craft *By Cindy Crandall-Frazier; Foreword by Linda Skolnik*
Will take you on a path deeper into your crocheting and your spiritual awareness.

The Knitting Way: A Guide to Spiritual Self-Discovery
By Linda Skolnick and Janice MacDaniels
Shows how to use the practice of knitting to strengthen our spiritual selves.

The Quilting Path: A Guide to Spiritual Self-Discovery through Fabric, Thread and Kabbalah *By Louise Silk*
Explores how to cultivate personal growth through quilt making.

The Painting Path: Embodying Spiritual Discovery through Yoga, Brush and Color *By Linda Novick; Foreword by Richard Segalman*
Explores the divine connection you can experience through art.

The Scrapbooking Journey: A Hands-On Guide to Spiritual Discovery
By Cory Richardson-Lauve; Foreword by Stacy Julian
Reveals how this craft can become a practice used to deepen and shape your life.

Travel

Israel—A Spiritual Travel Guide, 2nd Edition
A Companion for the Modern Jewish Pilgrim
By Rabbi Lawrence A. Hoffman
Also Available: **The Israel Mission Leader's Guide**

About Jewish Lights

People of all faiths and backgrounds yearn for books that attract, engage, educate, and spiritually inspire.

Our principal goal is to stimulate thought and help all people learn about who the Jewish People are, where they come from, and what the future can be made to hold. While people of our diverse Jewish heritage are the primary audience, our books speak to people in the Christian world as well and will broaden their understanding of Judaism and the roots of their own faith.

We bring to you authors who are at the forefront of spiritual thought and experience. While each has something different to say, they all say it in a voice that you can hear.

Our books are designed to welcome you and then to engage, stimulate, and inspire. We judge our success not only by whether or not our books are beautiful and commercially successful, but by whether or not they make a difference in your life.

For your information and convenience, at the back of this book we have provided a list of other Jewish Lights books you might find interesting and useful. They cover all the categories of your life:

Bar/Bat Mitzvah
Bible Study / Midrash
Children's Books
Congregation Resources
Current Events / History
Ecology / Environment
Fiction: Mystery, Science Fiction
Grief / Healing
Holidays / Holy Days
Inspiration
Kabbalah / Mysticism / Enneagram

Life Cycle
Meditation
Men's Interest
Parenting
Prayer / Ritual / Sacred Practice
Social Justice
Spirituality
Theology / Philosophy
Travel
12-Step
Women's Interest

Stuart M. Matlins, Publisher

Or phone, fax, mail or e-mail to: **JEWISH LIGHTS** Publishing
Sunset Farm Offices, Route 4 • P.O. Box 237 • Woodstock, Vermont 05091
Tel: (802) 457-4000 • Fax: (802) 457-4004 • www.jewishlights.com
Credit card orders: (800) 962-4544 (8:30AM–5:30PM ET Monday–Friday)
Generous discounts on quantity orders. SATISFACTION GUARANTEED. Prices subject to change.

The Jewish Contribution to Twelve Step Spirituality

An updated and expanded edition of a recovery classic. A rabbi, a psychiatrist, and many recovering Jewish people share their understanding of the Twelve Jewish Steps of recovery from addiction of all kinds based on conversations with each other—and with God.

They present a Jewish perspective on the Twelve Steps and offer consolation, inspiration, and motivation for recovery—for people of all faiths and backgrounds—by drawing on traditional and contemporary Jewish sources and by sharing what recovering people say about their experiences. They explore why some Jews are uncomfortable with the Twelve Steps, as well as how the Jewish understanding of the Twelve Steps differs from the Christian understanding of it.

Also Available from Jewish Lights

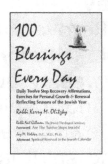

100 Blessings Every Day

Daily Twelve Step Recovery Affirmations, Exercises for Personal Growth & Renewal Reflecting Seasons of the Jewish Year
By Rabbi Kerry M. Olitzky; Foreword by Rabbi Neil Gillman
Using a one-day-at-a-time monthly format, reflects on the rhythm of the Jewish calendar with recovering people and other teachers, bringing insight to recovery from addictions and compulsive behaviors of all kinds.

Renewed Each Day
Daily Twelve Step Recovery Meditations
By Rabbi Kerry M. Olitzky and Aaron Z.
Using a seven-day/weekly guide format, a recovering person and a spiritual leader reflect on the traditional Jewish weekly Bible reading. They provide strong spiritual support for daily living and recovery from addictions of all kinds.
Vol.1—Genesis & Exodus

Introduction by Rabbi Michael A. Signer;
 Afterword by JACS Foundation
Vol.2—Leviticus, Numbers & Deuteronomy
Introduction by Sharon M. Strassfeld; Afterword
 by Rabbi Harold M. Schulweisar

Recovery from Codependence
A Jewish Twelve Steps Guide to Healing Your
 Soul
**By Rabbi Kerry M. Olitzky; Foreword by
 Marc Galanter, MD**
Afterword by Harriet Rossetto, LCSW
Explains how the Twelve Steps of
 Co-Dependents Anonymous are relevant for
Jewish people and all who would gain strength
to heal from Jewish tradition.

Rabbi Kerry M. Olitzky, DHL, is executive
director of the Jewish Outreach Institute. At the
forefront of Jewish education, he is the
organizer of many programs on chemical
dependency. He is the author of many books
on Jewish spirituality, healing, and Jewish

religious practice, including *100 Blessings Every Day: Daily Twelve Step Recovery Affirmations, Exercises for Personal Growth & Renewal Reflecting Seasons of the Jewish Year; Renewed Each Day: Daily Twelve Step Recovery Meditations Based on the Bible; Recovery from Codependence: A Jewish Twelve Steps Guide to Healing Your Soul;* and *Life's Daily Blessings: Inspiring Reflections on Gratitude and Joy for Every Day, Based on Jewish Wisdom* (all Jewish Lights).

Dr. Stuart A. Copans, board certified in addictions psychiatry, is adjunct associate professor of psychiatry at Dartmouth Medical School in Hanover, New Hampshire, and consulting child psychiatrist at Deerfield Academy and at Monadnock Family Services in Peterborough, New Hampshire. He is the author of many papers, abstracts, and other published works on the treatment of alcohol and drug abuse.

Dr. Abraham J. Twerski is a rabbi, psychiatrist, and an expert on recovery from addiction. He is medical director emeritus and founder of Gateway Rehabilitation Center in Aliquippa, Pennsylvania. Dr. Twerski is the author of many books on recovery and spirituality, including *The Spiritual Self: Getting Up When You're Down; Waking Up Just in Time; Self-Discovery in Recovery; Living Each Day;* and *A Formula for Proper Living: Practical Lessons from Life and Torah and Happiness and* *the Human Spirit: The Spirituality of Becoming the Best You Can Be* (both Jewish Lights).

Rabbi Sheldon Zimmerman founded the Task Force on Alcoholism of the Federation of Jewish Philanthropies of New York. While he was rabbi of Central Synagogue in New York City, his congregation sponsored the first Alcoholics Anonymous group to meet in a synagogue. Formerly president of Hebrew Union College–Jewish Institute of Religion, he is now rabbi of the Jewish Center of the Hamptons (NY).

Maty Grünberg is an Israeli artist who has made his home in London since the late 1960s. His illuminated books and sculptures are found in the collections of major museums and institutions throughout the world.

Also Available

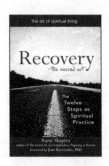

Recovery—The Sacred Art
The Twelve Steps as Spiritual Practice
By Rabbi Rami Shapiro; Foreword by Joan Borysenko, PhD

Deepen your capacity to live free from addiction—and from self and selfishness.

JEWISH LIGHTS Publishing
Sunset Farm Offices, Route 4, P.O. Box 237
Woodstock, VT 05091
Tel: (802) 457-4000
Fax: (802) 457-4004
www.jewishlights.com

BACK COVER MATERIAL

This book is not just for Jewish people.

It's for all people who would gain insight—and strength to heal—from Jewish tradition.

- All people who are in trouble with alcohol, drugs, or other addictions—food, gambling, and sex
- Anyone seeking an understanding of the Twelve Steps from a Jewish perspective—regardless of religious background or affiliation
- Alcoholics and addicts in recovery
- Codependents
- Adult children of alcoholics
- Specialists in recovery and treatment

"A powerful tool for spiritual transformation.... Guides all Jews seeking a Twelve-Step exodus from their personal enslavements to the promised land of freedom."
—Rabbi Rami Shapiro,
author, *Recovery—The Sacred Art: The Twelve Steps as Spiritual Practice*

"With honesty, compassion and hope ... weaves together the wisdom of AA Twelve Steps and Jewish teaching into a strong cord that ably pulls the reader out of the rut of compulsive behavior toward the freedom of responsible living."

—Rabbi Elie Kaplan Spitz,
author, *Healing from Despair: Choosing Wholeness in a Broken World*

"A 'must have' for any recovering person's library. Will help countless people begin the journey to a life of meaning and purpose, contentment and serenity. Our residents will all receive a copy as soon as they enter our doors."

—Martha J. Meehan,
executive director, Jewish Recovery Houses, Inc.

"Should be read by all people who are seeking meaning, purpose and a relevant spiritual path, whether they are officially recovering or not. The teachings reflect the essence of Jewish wisdom and are applicable to daily life. This book will be required reading for all residents of Beit T'Shuvah."

—Harriet Rossetto, LCSW,
founder and CEO, Beit T'Shuvah